Pontifications

The Naked and the Dead
Barbary Shore
The Deer Park
Advertisements for Myself
Deaths for the Ladies (and Other Disasters)
The Presidential Papers
An American Dream
Cannibals and Christians
Why Are We in Vietnam?
The Armies of the Night
Miami and the Siege of Chicago
Of a Fire on the Moon
The Prisoner of Sex
Existential Errands
St. George and the Godfather
Marilyn
The Fight
Genius and Lust
The Executioner's Song
Of Women and Their Elegance

NORMAN MAILER

Pontifications

INTERVIEWS
Edited by Michael Lennon

LITTLE, BROWN AND COMPANY   BOSTON · TORONTO

FIRST EDITION

LIBRARY OF CONGRESS CATALOG CARD NO. 82-082201

MV

Designed by Janis Capone

Published simultaneously in Canada
by Little, Brown & Company (Canada) Limited

PRINTED IN THE UNITED STATES OF AMERICA

Preface

❧

These interviews were put together through the labor of my friend, Michael Lennon, who searched them out and did much of the work of selecting them since there were something like one hundred interviews from which to choose. It is appropriate that he should write the introduction. By now, he knows more about these dialogues than I do. I wish only to say that we have one friendly but real disagreement. He ascribes value to my conversations and that is his right, but it is mine to shift my feet at the generosity of his praise.

I would add that "Pontifications" is a good description of what follows. In an interview, one answers the questions out of one's experience, out of the church — if the word may be allowed — of one's acquired knowledge. Logic may come in to serve your argument, and a fact can make its appearance now and then to bolster your reasoning, but the remarks are underwritten by experience. One's thought comes out as pronouncement — pontifications, indeed. And at their worst, these interviews can be pompous. But then pomposity clings as closely to pronouncement as a beer belly to a beer drinker.

It is obvious by these remarks that I am not fond of the form. I think an interview is truly an unhappy way to get it said, particularly for someone who speaks as poorly as I do. After years of hammering out consecutive sentences of reasonably good prose by dint of much repetition and reshaping of each phrase in my throat, before moving on to the next, I think the salt of good speech is leached out of one's mouth. When I write, I am forever going over the words. "Now, the best road, that is, the most agreeable, no, the most indigenous, say rather, the most comfortable to travel of all the roads to Burlington is, uh, that is, the road you are likely to find most agreeable, yes, the agreeable road . . ." Authors in raw transcript can seem as bad on occasion as politicians.

So I wince when I read over my remarks, I even improve them to a degree. There is hardly one of these interviews that was not edited by me years ago to get out the worst of the repetitions, and again for this book, and here and there — not too often — I have bolstered a few thoughts by a few after-the-fact phrases. You try to obtain a fair balance between the original tone, and the rights of the reader to respectable syntax, and you wince, as I say, you wince as you read your remarks, and true to your responsibility you keep most of the flat phrasing you would improve if committing such thoughts to writing.

Still, if you hold as I do to the notion that artists are not fond darlings of the universe who have been touched with talent the way certain women are blessed with beauty, but that, to the contrary, artists and beauties alike bear more resemblance to pack-horses carrying divine (or satanic) messages from one corner of our world to another, their talent or beauty only leased to them in order to do something interesting with it, then woe to those who don't. You can be certain there is a cry of failed endeavor behind every writer's interview, his mute apology for the book or the essay or the philosophy he did not achieve in the way he was meant to. Often, the particular answer is his last lunge as a relay runner. "Here," he gasps to the interlocutor, "is the message. Carry it to the reader. I am too pooped."

These interviews, from 1970 to 1981 (with excerpts from five earlier ones) take up, ergo, a number of questions I never developed to real satisfaction in my writing. They are part of the philosophy I promised myself to fashion and never did, never by formal means, and as the decades go by, and I come to recognize that I, too, can grow old, and never write all of what I thought I would, so, in resignation, I consign large parts of what I know to conversation.

One guide to the reader: Of the twenty interviews reprinted here, five — the first five — were given in the years from 1958 to 1967. Since four of them can be found in my other collections, they have been cut approximately by half for inclusion in this book, and would have been passed over if not for the foundation they provide. Just about all the matters that are discussed in later interviews have their origins here. Besides — as Lennon points out, interviewers can be like chess players "aware of the games of their predecessors" — and so these early exchanges while overdramatic, and excessive in language, are probably worth including for their undeniable relevance.

Contents

Pontifications

❦

.

Introduction

by Michael Lennon

❧

I think Gertrude Stein may have been too sweeping when she said to Hemingway, "Remarks are not literature." It depends. Hemingway's remarks in his 1958 interview in *The Paris Review* certainly qualify, and several of the interviews with Norman Mailer collected here are of comparable stature. Collectively, these twenty interviews express his views on every subject close to his concern for the past quarter of a century. If these selected conversations with friends, journalists, academics and students are not literature, not certifiably a formal part of Mailer's literary work, they are at the least, an indispensable adjunct to it.

On some subjects — pornography, drugs, marriage, his books, his career, his theology and the psychological stances involved in writing a novel — the interviews may even be accorded the status of the major biographical sources. But they are to be recommended for more than the exportable information that they provide. As a literary form, the interview has much to offer someone of Mailer's temperament. As sensitive to mood as Hemingway, he has been more willing than his old mentor to exercise that portion of himself most serviceable for the occasion. The chemistry between Mailer and his different interlocutors stimulates him to a variety of conversational gambits: elucidative, admonitory, quasi-confessional, speculative and, of course, forensic. Since Hemingway's death Mailer has been the literary world's finest counterpuncher, although he displays none of Hemingway's archness (or Faulkner's sullenness). He does unload a few good, solid antipathies though: corporate America, plastics, the FBI and modern architecture. His method is more dialectical than peremptory, however. Indeed, the interviews bear some resemblance to a twenty-five-year chess match, new players (most of whom are aware of the games of their predecessors) succeeding old, and Mailer adapting his tactics for each. A great part of the pleasure the interviews provide lies in the opportunity to savor the various gambits Mailer employs, and to watch for the signs of change in his ideas. Even when an interviewer appears to have summed up some aspect of Mailer's thought or art, he resists in favor of a more subtle formulation. Occasionally he asks the questions; at other times he plays devil's advocate and notes the weakness of his own position, stating it earlier or more firmly than his interviewer, a tactic he mastered in *The Armies of the Night*. He enjoys a fast, tough exchange (the one with Anita Eichholz in "A Brief Exchange," on the question of the Women's Liberation movement, for example, which is the perfect pendant to *The Prisoner of Sex*); it seems to notch his own thinking higher. His ego, which he once compared to an egg, is more like a golf ball — the harder it is hit, the more lively it becomes. He finds artful ways to answer uninformed questions and can usually find a decent peg on which to hang an answer to imprecise ones. An excellent listener, he seems to deploy just enough acumen to raise the discussion one rung higher and he never tries to embarrass. So he will answer dull questions with a modicum of wit, turn intellectual batteries on academics who know his work well and use his knowledge of old-friend interviewers where it will be helpful. In sum, he is a great talker.

Paradoxically, the final worth of these interviews may reside in the fact that Mailer is suspicious of the form. Because he believes that there is an umbilical relation between good thinking, good writing and mild depression, his first instinct is to be skeptical of any idea that comes too easily, or too enthusiastically. The insight has been well endowed by experience. Imagine then his mistrust of ideas that arise in casual conversation. Consequently, he works to maintain the life of the discussion at its highest possible level. Advancing the argument is more important than making points.

Mailer is, among many other things, an unfrocked prophet, full of foreboding about contemporary American culture, and this collection shows how he has gone about this business. In the earlier interviews, especially, he barnstorms through familiar territory: the sexual revolution, drugs, technology, violence, the media, God and the

Devil, the death of the romantic spirit, American politics, existentialism and the various forms of totalitarianism, "displaying," as Robert F. Lucid once noted, "a hundred different moods and attitudes when he is in them, above all trying always to evoke the essence of the moment through his endless conjuring of metaphor."

In the later interviews Mailer's range is even greater, and he is just as concerned to refine his metaphors, but he is more conjectural. His ideas have changed over the years, of course, significantly in some cases, but then so has the country. Yet the changes in his emphases have never been purely reflexive. Mailer chooses his targets, and his arrows, with care. If he has no idiosyncratic insight or perspective on a matter, he passes, which partly explains why his most controversial remarks are often his most serious. If he cannot inform he won't provoke. His goal is to tell us how the world works. In this sense, he is still a realist in the tradition of Zola and Dos Passos.

In the late Eisenhower period Mailer billed himself as a "psychic outlaw." Thirteen years later during the Nixon–McGovern campaign, a "modest and half-invisible Aquarius" vibrated in the winds of the *Zeitgeist*. These are the extremes that are represented in these interviews. Compare for example the all-out slugging exchanges with Krassner in 1962 with the reflective conversation he has with McElroy and a group of writing students at Columbia University in 1981. In the earlier interview "the subjects grind by like boxcars on a two-mile freight," as Mailer later put it. In the Columbia interview, he proceeds with Jamesian deliberation, lingers actually, in his discussion of the lore and craft of novel-writing, admitting uncertainties, offering suggestions and making subtle forays into an area at the edge of the word system: the mysterious powers of ego and identity that have sustained him in his life as a writer. Mailer is considerably more intrigued with questions of craft and style in the recent interviews than he was, for example, in the 1963 interview with Marcus, perhaps for no better reason than he has now lived the writer's life for twice as long, over forty years.

Each interview illumines some moment of his career and most cover a multitude of topics (the 1967 interview with Carroll and the Munich conversations he conducted with me in 1980 come closest to being synopticons of his views). Even those with similar subjects (with Farbar, for example, in 1973, Medwick in 1980 and Michelson/Stone in 1981 on sex, love and marriage; and with Stern in 1958, Stratton in 1974 and Adams in 1975 on God and the Devil) are markedly different. Some of the interviews, moreover, offer

Mailer's most important or only substantial utterance on a major topic and so have their claim to interest. His long discussion of pornography in the Michelson/Stone interview is one; the portions of the 1970 Young interview in which he explores the primitive sensibility is another. A third is his conversation with Stratton on Charles Manson and rock music. Several of the interviews contain unrehearsed and incisive comment on writers, or "fellow racketeers," as he calls them, that he has discussed little or not at all before: Borges, Márquez, Hannah Arendt, Doctorow, Tom Wolfe and Ann Beattie. There are also some surprising remarks on writers he has had on his mind for decades: Marx, Freud, Hemingway, Faulkner, Fitzgerald and Sartre. Speckled throughout are asides and quick references to many more: Kafka, Forster, Burroughs, Penn Warren, Steinbeck, Graham Greene, Heller, Nin, Tolstoy and Dostoyevsky, Porter, Capote, Durrell, Fowles and Raymond Chandler. The 1980 interview with Attanasio is notable for its capsule discussions of writers. (Note: Dates given here and at the end of each interview refer to the years the interviews were conducted, not the years of first publication.)

In the earliest interview presented here, his 1958 dialogue with Stern on his unique theology, Mailer begins by saying, "I started as one kind of writer and I've been evolving into another kind." Over the twenty-four-year period (1958–1981) from which these interviews are drawn, Mailer has become another kind of writer at least three times. The first metamorphosis came a year after the Stern interview with the publication of *Advertisements for Myself*. There, he dropped all pretense of separating his personal and creative lives and candidly dissected his achievements, failures and ambitions. The second was revealed nine years later in *The Armies of the Night*, in which he describes his former self in the third person, thus casting his outspoken public persona into sharp relief. Mailer used this unusual point of view in the four nonfiction narratives he published after *Armies*, all of which are personal testaments of the public life of the nation during the period from 1967–72. If the Sixties could be considered Mailer's autobiographical decade, the Seventies may fairly be called his biographical period. After the 1972 elections he all but lost interest in himself as a protagonist and devoted the rest of the decade to a series of works on famous-infamous Americans: Marilyn Monroe (*Marilyn: A Novel Biography*, 1973); Muhammad Ali (*The Fight*, 1975); Henry Miller (*Genius and Lust*, 1977); Gary Gilmore (*The Executioner's Song*, 1979); and Marilyn again in *Of Women and Their Elegance,* published in 1980. These four figures, and their narcissistic obsessions, are discussed in several of the interviews from 1974 on.

Mailer is now poised for another change, by his own estimate perhaps the largest. From reports of his public readings from the huge novel set in ancient Egypt that he has been working on since 1971, it seems likely that its publication in a year or two will reveal still another kind of writer. For the first time, it looks as if we will encounter the author trying to get outside of both history and personality — to get so far back in time as to stop it, to imagine human society in a time and place where historical memory cannot reach. He makes a number of tantalizing comments on this long-awaited novel in several of the later interviews, and also explains why he is usually unwilling to discuss his fictional, as opposed to his nonfictional, work-in-progress.

Novelists, Mailer says, must believe that words can change lives — if they are good enough. So words are best devoted to novels. Agreed; and there is where our chief interest will be. But if we wish to glimpse the process as well as read the product, these conversations may be the best place to look.

Hip, Hell
and the Navigator

An Interview
with Richard G. Stern and Robert Lucid

❧

RICHARD STERN: I've been reading "The White Negro" and a fair amount of other material on the hipster, and I must say that intellectually I resent Hip as much as I can resent anything. Now I wonder about the extent of your allegiance to Hip. Are you using this material for fiction, or are you committed to it as a style of life, one which you want to practice yourself and recommend to others?

NORMAN MAILER: All right, good, I think the difficulty for most people who are at all interested in my work is that I started as one kind of writer, and I've been evolving into another. Most serious readers like a writer to be a particular thing. It's important; it's reassuring, somehow. So, I think if I'm going in this direction, it has to be assumed at least from the outside that I'm serious.

STERN: The interesting thing about Hip is that Hip shouldn't belong to writers. If you're a genuine hipster you're committed, it seems to me, to a kind of anti-expressionism. If you're a sincere hipster you shouldn't be a writer. Then there's another thing as far as writing goes. Isn't a novel controlled by some overriding notion, by a kind of fanaticism which organizes a great deal of disparate material? In a sense, a novel is like the mind of a madman: everything — casual looks, street signs, world news reports — is charged with meaning. That's why novelists write about ruling passions like love and ambition, passions which put their mark on all they touch, trivial or major. Now I can't believe that Hip allows for such overriding notions and passions. For the hipster, the cool one, detail is illumined, livid, but for its own sake, unqualified by the sort of organization which novels demand. I wonder if such material can be put into fiction.

MAILER: I think it can; and not only that, but I think Hip is particularly illumined by one notion so central and so shattering that its religious resonances and reverberations are going to dominate this coming century. And I think there is one single burning pinpoint of the vision in Hip: it's that God is in danger of dying. In my very limited knowledge of theology, this never really has been expressed before. I believe Hip conceives of Man's fate being tied up with God's fate. God is no longer all-powerful.

STERN: Now that's a fantastic assertion. That really makes me sit up. What is the notion of God behind all this? Do you mean that some kind of personal god is dying with us?

MAILER: Now I only talk about my own vision of it, really. I think that the particular God we can conceive of is a god whose relationship to the universe we cannot divine; that is, how enormous He is in the scheme of the universe we can't begin to say. But almost certainly, He is not all-powerful; He exists as a warring element in a divided universe, and we are a part of — perhaps the most important part of — His great expression, His enormous destiny; perhaps He is trying to impose upon the universe His conception of being against other conceptions of being very much opposed to His. Maybe we are in a sense the seed, the seed-carriers, the voyagers, the explorers, the embodiment of that embattled vision; maybe we are engaged in a heroic activity, and not a mean one.

STERN: This is really something.

MAILER: Well, I would say it is far more noble in its conception, far more arduous as a religious conception than the notion of the all-powerful God who takes care of us.

STERN: And do you take to this conception for its perilous nobility, or do you take to it because you believe in it?

MAILER: I believe in it.

STERN: You believe in it.

MAILER: It's the only thing that makes any sense to me. It's the only thing that explains to me the problem of evil. You see, the answer may well be — how to put it? — that God Himself is engaged in a destiny so extraordinary, so demanding, that He too can suffer from a moral corruption, that He can make demands upon us which are unfair, that He can abuse our beings in order to achieve His means, even as we abuse the very cells of our own body.

STERN: Is it a person's duty to find out whether he's of God's party, whether he's working with God-beneficent or God-maleficent?

MAILER: Well, look, let's go back; let's go back to something much more modest for the moment which I think may tie this up, to a small extent, anyway. You asked me before why Hip is interesting for the novel. Well, up to now, when a novelist treats someone like a drug addict, the Square way is to treat the addict as a poor sociological cripple who is doomed and damned and goes down to his inevitable defeat. In Hip, which has after all to a certain extent come out of drug-taking (it's one of the elements in the growth of Hip) the attitude would be more that if taking drugs gives one extraordinary sensations, then the drug-taker is probably receiving something from God. Love perhaps. And perhaps he is. Let's just entertain the notion as a rational hypothesis which may or may not be true and let's see how far we go with it. If the hipster is receiving love from God he may well be draining some of the substance of God by calling upon this love, you see, which the drug releases. And in draining the substance of God he's exhausting Him, so that the drug-taker may be indulging an extraordinarily evil act at the instant he is filled with the feeling that he is full of God and good and a beautiful mystic. This involves new moral complexities which I feel are far more interesting than anything the novel has gotten into yet. It opens the possibility that the novel, along with many other art forms, may be growing into something larger rather than something smaller, and the sickness of our times for me has been just this damn thing that everything has been getting smaller and smaller and less and less important, that the romantic spirit has dried up, that there is almost no shame today like the terror before the romantic. We're all getting so mean and small and petty and ridiculous, and we all live under the threat of extermination. In contrast, the notions of Hip enlarge us, they make our small actions not necessarily large, but more meaningful. If we pick up a bottle while listening to some jazz and we feel each of our five fingertips in relation to the bottle, the bottle begins to have a kind of form for us and we begin to feel each of our fingertips is receiving a different thing from the shape and the structure of the glass, and we then begin to think that maybe the very structure of this glass could conceivably contain some kind of hell within its constitution, some inorganic frozen state of imprisoned being less being than us. I think it's a more interesting notion that just picking up a bottle and pouring out some whisky.

STERN: It's a very pretty notion.

MAILER: Hip is pretty.

STERN: But it's all action, it's all erectile, isn't it? It's all feeling and taste and touch and smell. Isn't that the trouble with it?

MAILER: The trouble is that it's enormously <u>difficult to return to the senses</u>. We're all civilized, and to return to the senses and keep the best parts of our civilized being, to keep our capacity for mental organization, for mental construction, for logic, is doubly difficult, and there's a great danger that the nihilism of Hip will destroy civilization. But it seems to me that the danger which is even more paramount — the danger which has brought on Hip — is that civilization is so strong itself, so divorced from the senses, that we have come to the point where we can liquidate millions of people in concentration camps by orderly process.

STERN: Every powerful and refining force involves danger and waste. Does this divorce from the senses you talk about justify cashing in two or three thousand years of continuous culture?

MAILER: Well, your argument is moot. It's too vast for this — for me. But let me try to put it this way. If the divorce from the senses I talk about is becoming a human condition, then by all means, yes, civilization must be cashed in or we will destroy ourselves in the <u>cold insensate expressions</u> of <u>due process of law and atomic radiation</u>.

STERN: All right, let's concentrate on what all this has to do with you as a practicing novelist. How are these notions going to work for you? The idea of art seems to me to be to generate emotion from the treated material, not to point out some material and some feeling and say, "Put them together, reader."

MAILER: Well, let me avoid answering you directly. I feel that the final purpose of art is to <u>intensify, even</u>, <u>if necessary, to exacerbate, the moral consciousness of peo</u>ple. In particular, I think the novel is at its best the most moral of the art forms because it's the most immediate, the most overbearing, if you will. It is the most inescapable. Ideally, what I would hope to do with my work is intensify a consciousness that the core of life cannot be cheated. <u>Every moment of one's existence one is growing into more or retreating into less. One is always living a little more or dying a little bit</u>. That the choice is not to live a little more or to not live a

little more; it is to live a little more or to die a little more. And as
one dies a little more, one enters a most dangerous moral condition for oneself because one starts making other people die a little
more in order to stay alive oneself. I think this is exactly the murderous network in which we all live by now.

STERN: And this is what the hipster does; he strikes out at others;
he's constantly craving for more. He faces the risk of the extinction of his senses, extinction of his being, extinction of his capacity for making distinctions.

MAILER: He does certain things that are very brave in their way; he
gambles for one thing with his soul — he gambles that he can be
terribly, tragically wrong, and therefore be doomed, you see,
doomed to Hell. Which the churchy people don't do at all.
They're thinking of nothing but maintaining their souls for some
careful preservation afterward. The hipster is gambling with
death and he is gambling with the Hereafter; and he may be
wrong.

STERN: And the novelist is gambling with his talent as a novelist.

MAILER: Oh, yeah. Yeah.

STERN: The one talent he's got.

ROBERT LUCID: This is what kills me. You presume consciousness,
you presume purpose, you presume direction on the part of this
class — if that's the word — analogous to the novelist. And it
seems to me that the whole notion of Hip is, in fact, unconscious,
it is mere action. It seems to me the kind of guy we're talking
about as hipster *qua* hipster is a guy who is, in fact, unconscious
of risks of this kind, of the profundity . . .

MAILER: Consciously, he may think it's cutting quite a few corners
as far as that goes. What I'm postulating in all this — the notion
I've been working with all along that's been tacit to my remarks,
implicit in my remarks, is that the unconscious, you see, has an
enormous teleological sense, that it moves towards a goal, that it
has a real sense of what is happening to one's being at each given
moment — you see — that the messages of one's experience are
continually saying, "Things are getting better," or "Things are
getting worse." For me. For that one. For my future, for my past,
mmm? It is with this thing that they move, that they grope
forward — this navigator at the seat of their being.

1958

An Impolite Interview

An Interview with Paul Krassner

❧

PAUL KRASSNER: When you and I first talked about the possibility of doing an impolite interview, we kind of put it off because you said: "I find that when I discuss ideas, it spills the tension I need to write." Which seems like a very Freudian explanation. Does it still apply?

NORMAN MAILER: It does. Sure it does. I think putting out half-worked ideas in an interview is like premature ejaculation.

KRASSNER: Then why bother?

MAILER: I'm beginning to get a little pessimistic about the number of ideas I never write up. Perhaps the public is better off with premature ejaculation than no intellectual sex at all. I'm just thinking of the public, not myself.

KRASSNER: All right, you once referred in passing to the FBI as a religious movement: would you elaborate on that?

MAILER: I think a lot of people need the FBI for their sanity. That is to say, in order to be profoundly religious, to become a saint, for example, one must dare insanity, but if one wishes instead to flee from insanity, then one method is to join an organized religion. The FBI is an organized religion.

    The FBI blots out everything which could bring dread into the average mediocrity's life. At bottom, I mean profoundly at bottom, the FBI has nothing to do with Communism, it has nothing to do with catching criminals, it has nothing to do with the Mafia, the Syndicate, it has nothing to do with trustbusting, it has nothing to do with interstate commerce, it has nothing to do with anything but serving as a church for the mediocre. A high church for the true mediocre.

KRASSNER: In terms of the mass media being a force to which one subjects oneself more voluntarily than to the FBI, isn't it possible that the mass media which you call totalitarian are a reflection rather than a cause of this condition in society?

MAILER: A reflection of what people want? No, I don't think so. That's like saying that the United States Army was a reflection of what the soldiers wanted.

KRASSNER: But they were drafted —

MAILER: And you're not drafted — your eye is not *drafted* when you turn on that TV set? To assume that people are getting what they want through the mass media also assumes that the men and women who direct the mass media know something about the people. But they don't know anything about the people. That's why I gave you the example of the Army. The private exists in a world which is hermetically alienated from the larger aims of the generals who are planning the higher strategy of the war.

The mass media is made up of a group of people who are looking for power. The reason is not because they have any moral sense, any inner sense of a goal, of an ideal that's worth fighting ✳ for, dying for, if one is brave enough. No, the reason they want power is because power is the only thing that will relieve the profound illness which has seized them. Which has seized all of us. The illness of the twentieth century. There isn't psychic room for all of us. Malthus's law has moved from the excessive procreation of bodies to the excessive mediocritization of psyches. The deaths don't occur on the battlefield any longer, or through malnutrition: they occur within the brain, within the psyche itself.

KRASSNER: To change the subject: Several months ago I mentioned, in order to make a very definite point, a Cuban prostitute — this was the first prostitute I'd ever gone to, and I had been asking her all these questions about the Revolution — and she stopped later in the middle of fellatio to ask me if I was a Communist.

MAILER: You were in Cuba at the time?

KRASSNER: Yes. And she was anti-Castro.

MAILER: Because he was cleaning them out of the whorehouses?

KRASSNER: Well, there were no more tourists coming to Cuba, and it was ruining their business. Anyway, I described this incident in the *Realist*, and was accused of exhibitionism by some friends of mine. And I'm secure enough in my life that I had no need to boast about this; but it was a funny, significant thing which I wanted to share with the readers.

MAILER: Oh, I remember that, I remember reading your piece now. I was a little shocked by it.

KRASSNER: You're kidding.

MAILER: No, I was shocked. I wasn't profoundly shocked. It threw me slightly. I had a feeling, "That's not good writing." And the next thought was, "Mailer, you're getting old." And the next thought was, "If you're not really getting old, but there is something indeed bad about this writing, what is it that's bad about it?"

KRASSNER: And?

MAILER: A whore practicing fellatio looks up and says, "Are you a Communist?" — that's what the modern world is all about in a way. Saying it head-on like that probably gave the atmosphere honesty. But, in some funny way, it didn't belong.

If the reader had been able to guess that this was what was going on with the whore — I don't know how you could have done it; that would have been the art of it — to phrase the language in such a way that the reader thinks, "Oh, Jesus, she's sucking his cock, and she asks him if he's a Communist." If it had happened that way, it might have been overpowering. What a montage.

Maybe it was the use of "fellatio," maybe you just should have said, "I was having my cock sucked and she said, 'Are you a Communist?' " If you're getting into the brutality of it, get into the brutality of it. Throw a beanball. Don't use the Latinism. Maybe it was the Latinism that threw me. All I know is that there was something bad about it, the effect was *shock*.

KRASSNER: So you were shocked by a euphemism . . .

MAILER: Shock is like banging your head or taking a dull fall; your wits are deadened.

KRASSNER: That's what I wanted to do in the writing, because that's what happened to me in the act.

MAILER: Then you're not interested in art, you're interested in therapy. That's the trouble — there are too many people writing nowadays who give no art to the world, but draw in therapy to themselves.

KRASSNER: No, not in my case. It didn't change me one way or the other, writing it. I just wanted to put it into the consciousness of the reader. That's not therapy for me.

MAILER: Well, then you should've said, "She was sucking my cock." I mean that's my professional opinion.

KRASSNER: If you were a future historian of sex, how would you look upon the Kennedy administration?

MAILER: I'd say there's more acceptance of sexuality in America today than there was before he came in. Whether that's good or bad, I don't know. It may be a promiscuous acceptance of sexuality.

KRASSNER: Are you saying it's because of. . . ?

MAILER: Because of Kennedy — *absolutely.* I mean, just think of going to a party given by Eisenhower as opposed to a party thrown by Kennedy. Do you have to wonder at which party you'd have a better time?

The average man daydreams about his leader. He thinks of being invited to his leader's home. If he thinks of being invited to Eisenhower's home, he thinks of how proper he's going to be. If he thinks of going to the Kennedys for a party, he thinks of having a dance with Jackie. Things liven up.

Why do you think people loved Hitler in Germany? Because they all secretly wished to get hysterical and *stomp* on things and scream and shout and rip things up and *kill* — tear people apart. Hitler pretended to offer them that. In some subtle way, he communicated it. That's why they wanted him. That's why he was good for Germany — they wanted such horror. Of course, by the end he didn't tear people apart, he gassed them.

If America gets as sick as Germany was before Hitler came in, we'll have our Hitler. One way or another, we'll have our Hitler. After all, one can have Fascism come in any form at all, through the Church, through sex, through social welfare, through state conservatism, through organized medicine, the FBI, the Pentagon. Fascism is not a philosophy but a <u>murderous mode of deadening reality by smothering it with lies</u>.

Every time one sees a bad television show, one is watching the nation get ready for the day when a Hitler will come. Not because the ideology of the show is Fascistic; on the contrary its manifest ideology is invariably liberal, but the show still prepares Fascism because it is meretricious art and so sickens people a little further. Whenever people get collectively sick, the remedy becomes progressively more violent and hideous. An insidious, insipid sickness demands a violent far-reaching purgative.

KRASSNER: Then you're saying it's bad times which result in bad leaders.

MAILER: Well, if a time is bad enough, a good man can't possibly succeed. In a bad time, the desires of the multitude are bad, they're low, they're ugly, they're greedy, they're cowardly, they're piggish, shitty.

KRASSNER: In *The Naked and the Dead*, there was a theme about the futility of violence on a grand scale; and yet, in "The White Negro," there's almost a justification of violence, at least on a personal level. How do you reconcile this apparent inconsistency?

MAILER: What I still disapprove of is *inhuman* violence — violence which is on a large scale and abstract. I disapprove of bombing a city. I disapprove of the kind of man who will derive aesthetic satisfaction from the fact that an Ethiopian village looks like a red rose at the moment the bombs are exploding. I won't disapprove of the act of perception which witnesses that; I think that act of perception is — I'm going to use the word again — noble.

What I'm getting at is: a native village is bombed, and the bombs happen to be beautiful when they land; in fact it would be odd if all that sudden destruction did not liberate some beauty. The form a bomb takes in its explosion may be in part a picture of the potentialities it destroyed. So let us accept the idea that the bomb is beautiful.

If so, any liberal who decries the act of bombing is totalitarian if he doesn't admit as well that the bombs were indeed beautiful.

Because the moment we tell something that's untrue, it does not matter how pure our motives may be — the moment we start mothering mankind and decide that one truth is good for them to hear and another is not so good, because while *we* can understand, those poor ignorant unfortunates cannot — then what are we doing, we're depriving the minds of others of knowledge which may be essential.

Think of a young pilot who comes along later, some young pilot who goes out on a mission and isn't prepared for the fact that a bombing might be beautiful; he could conceivably be an idealist, there were some in the war against Fascism. If the pilot is totally unprepared he might never get over the fact that he was particularly thrilled by the beauty of that bomb.

But if our culture had been large enough to say that Ciano's son-in-law not only found that bomb beautiful, but that indeed this act of perception was *not* what was wrong; the evil was to think that this beauty was worth the lot of living helpless people who were wiped out broadside. Obviously, whenever there's destruction, there's going to be beauty implicit in it.

KRASSNER: Do you think you're something of a puritan when it comes to masturbation?

MAILER: I think masturbation is bad.

KRASSNER: In relation to heterosexual fulfillment?

MAILER: In relation to everything — orgasm, heterosexuality, to style, to stance, to be able to fight the good fight. I think masturbation cripples people. It doesn't cripple them altogether, but it turns them askew, it sets up a bad and often enduring tension. I mean has anyone ever studied the correlation between cigarette smoking and masturbation? Anybody who spends his adolescence masturbating, generally enters his young manhood with no sense of being a man. The answer — I don't know what the answer is — sex for adolescents may be the answer, it may not. I really don't know.

KRASSNER: Is it possible that you have a totalitarian attitude against masturbation?

MAILER: I wouldn't say all people who masturbate are evil, probably I would even say that some of the best people in the world masturbate. But I am saying it's a miserable activity.

KRASSNER: Well, we're getting right back now to this notion of absolutes. You know — to somebody, masturbation can be a thing of beauty —

MAILER: To what end? To what end? Who is going to benefit from it?

KRASSNER: It's a better end than the beauty of a bombing.

MAILER: Masturbation is bombing. It's bombing oneself.

KRASSNER: I think there's a basic flaw in your argument. Why are you assuming that masturbation is violence unto oneself? Why is it not pleasure unto oneself? And I'm not defending masturbation — well, I'm defending masturbation, yes, as a substitute if and when —

MAILER: All right, look. When you make love, whatever is good in you or bad in you, goes out into someone else. I mean this literally. I'm not interested in the biochemistry of it, the electromagnetism of it, nor in how the psychic waves are passed back and forth, and what psychic waves are. All I know is that when one makes love, one changes a woman slightly and a woman changes you slightly.

KRASSNER: Certain circumstances can change one for the worse.

MAILER: But at least you have gone through a process which is part of life. One can be better for the experience, or worse. But one has experience to absorb, to think about, one has literally to digest the new spirit which has entered the flesh. The body has been galvanized for an experience of flesh, a declaration of the flesh.

If one has the courage to think about every aspect of the act — I don't mean think mechanically about it, but if one is able to brood over the act, to dwell on it — then one is *changed* by the act. Even if one has been *jangled* by the act. Because in the act of restoring one's harmony, one has to encounter all the reasons one was jangled.

So finally one has had an experience which is nourishing. Nourishing because one's able to *feel* one's way into more difficult or more precious insights as a result of it. One's able to live a tougher, more heroic life if one can digest and absorb the experience.

But, if one masturbates, all that happens is, everything that's beautiful and good in one, goes up the hand, goes into the air, is *lost.* Now what the hell is there to *absorb?* One hasn't tested himself. You see, in a way, the heterosexual act lays questions to rest, and makes one able to build upon a few answers. Whereas if one masturbates, the ability to contemplate one's experience is disturbed. Instead, fantasies of power take over and disturb all sleep.

If one has, for example, the image of a beautiful sexy babe in masturbation, one still doesn't know whether one can make love to her in the flesh. All you know is that you can violate her in your *brain.* Well, a lot of good that is.

But if one has fought the good fight or the evil fight and ended with the beautiful sexy dame, then if the experience is good, your life is changed by it, in a less happy way. But at least one knows something of what happened. One has something real to build on.

The ultimate direction of masturbation always has to be insanity.

KRASSNER: But you're not man enough to take the other position, which is sex for the young. Except for petting, what else is there between those two alternatives?

MAILER: I'd say, between masturbation and sex for the young, I prefer sex for the young. Of course. But I think there may be still a

third alternative: At the time I grew up, sex had enormous fascination for everyone, but it had no dignity, it had no place. It was
not a value. It had nothing to do with procreation, it had to do
with the bathroom — it was burning, it was feverish, it was dirty,
cute, giggly.

The thought of waiting for sex never occurred — when I was
young my parents did not speak about sex, and no one else I knew
ever discussed the possibility of holding on to one's sex as the
single most important thing one has. To keep one's sex until one
got what one deserved for it — that was never suggested to me
when I was young.

The possibilities were to go out and have sex with a girl, have
homosexual sex, or masturbate. Those were the choices. The
fourth alternative — chastity, if you will — was ridiculous and
absurd. It's probably more absurd today. If you talked to kids of
chastity today, they would not stop laughing, I'm certain.

But the fact of the matter is, if you get marvelous sex when
you're young, all right; but if you're not ready to make a baby
with that marvelous sex, then you may also be putting something
down the drain forever, which is the ability that you had to make
a baby; the most marvelous thing that was in you may have been
shot into a diaphragm, or wasted on a pill. One might be losing
one's future.

The point is that, so long as one has a determinedly atheistic
and rational approach to life, then the only thing that makes sense
is the most comprehensive promiscuous sex you can find.

KRASSNER: Well, since I do have an essentially atheistic and more-
or-less rational approach to life, I think I can speak with at least
my individual authority. As a matter of fact, the more rational I
become, the more selective —

MAILER: You know, "selective" is a word that sounds like a refugee
from a group therapy session.

KRASSNER: I've never been in any kind of therapy —

MAILER: No, I know, but there's a *plague* coming out of all these
centers — they go around *infecting* all of us. The words sit in
one's vocabulary like bedbugs under glass.

KRASSNER: But I can't think of a better word. "Selective" is a word
that means what I want to communicate to you.

MAILER: Selective. It's arrogant — how do you know who's doing
the selecting? I mean you're a modest man with a good sense of
yourself, but suddenly it comes to sex and you're selective. Like
you won't pick *this* girl; you'll pick *that* one.

KRASSNER: Exactly. It's arrogant, but —

MAILER: Yeah, yeah, yeah — but the fact that one girl wants you and the other girl *doesn't* — I mean, that has nothing to do with it?

KRASSNER: Well, they have a right to be selective, too.

MAILER: Then it's mutually selective.

KRASSNER: Well, what I'm saying is you make a choice. A human choice. It has nothing to do with a machine . . . I'll tell you what's bugging me — it's your mystical approach. You'll use an expression like "You may be sending the best baby that's in you out into you hand" — but even when you're having intercourse, how many unused spermatozoa will there be in one ejaculation of semen?

MAILER: Look, America is dominated by a bunch of half-maniacal scientists, men who don't know anything about the act of creation. If science comes along and says there are one million spermatozoa in a discharge, you reason on that basis. That may not be a real basis.

We just don't know what the *real* is. We just don't know. Of the million spermatozoa, there may be only two or three with any real chance of reaching the ovum; the others are there like a supporting army, or if we're talking of planned parenthood, as a body of the electorate. These sperm go out with no sense at all of being real spermatozoa. They may appear to be real spermatozoa under the microscope, but after all, a man from Mars who's looking at us through a telescope might think that Communist bureaucrats and FBI men look exactly the same.

KRASSNER: Well, they are.

MAILER: Krassner's jab piles up more points. The point is that the scientists don't know what's going on. That meeting of the ovum and the sperm is too mysterious for the laboratory. Even the electron microscope can't measure the striations of passion in a spermatozoon. Or the force of its will.

But we can trust our emotion. Our emotions are a better guide to what goes on in these matters than scientists.

Sooner or later, every man comes close to his being and realizes that even though he's using the act, the act is using him too. He becomes, as you say, more selective. The reason he becomes more selective is that you can get killed, you literally *can* fuck your head off, you can lose your brains, you can wreck your body, you can use yourself up badly, eternally — I know a little bit of what I'm talking about.

KRASSNER: In his book *Nobody Knows My Name*, James Baldwin — referring to your essay "The White Negro" — complained about "the myth of the sexuality of Negroes which Norman Mailer, like so many others, refuses to give up." Are you still denying it's a myth?

MAILER: I don't believe it's a myth at all, for any numbers of reasons. I think that *any* submerged class is going to be more accustomed to sexuality than a leisure class. A leisure class may be more *preoccupied* with sexuality; but a submerged class is going to be more drenched in it.

You see, the upper classes are obsessed with sex, but they contain very little of it themselves. They use up much too much sex in their manipulations of power. In effect, they exchange sex for power. They restrict themselves in their sexuality — whereas the submerged classes have to take their desires for power and plow them back into sex.

So, to begin with, there's just that much more sexual vitality at the bottom than there is at the top. Second of all, the Negroes come from Africa, which is more or less a tropical land. It's easier to cohabit, it's easier to stay alive. If there's more time, more leisure, more warmth, more — we'll use one of those machine words — more support-from-the-environment than there is in a Northern country, then sex will tend to be more luxuriant.

Northern countries try to build civilizations and tropical countries seek to proliferate *being*.

Besides, the Negro has been all but forbidden any sort of intellectual occupation here for a couple of centuries. So he has had to learn other ways of comprehending modern life. There are two ways one can get along in the world. One can get along by studying books, or one can get along by knowing a great deal about one's fellow man, and one's fellow man's woman.

Sexuality is the armature of Negro life. Without sexuality they would've perished. The Jews stayed alive by having a culture to which they could refer, in which, more or less, they could believe. The Negroes stayed alive by having sexuality which could nourish them, keep them warm.

KRASSNER: Would you say that your conception of life is mystical as opposed to rationalistic?

MAILER: I don't like to call myself a mystic. On the other hand, I certainly wouldn't classify myself as a rationalist. I'm not altogether unhappy living in some no-man's-land between the two.

KRASSNER: OK, final question: You beat me two out of three times in thumb-wrestling matches; would you care to expound briefly on Zen in the art of thumb-wrestling?

MAILER: They are the same.

1962

Craft and Consciousness

An Interview with Steven Marcus

☙

STEVEN MARCUS: Would you say something about style, prose style, in relation to the novel?

NORMAN MAILER: A really good style comes only when a man has become as good as he can be. Style is character. A good style cannot come from a bad undisciplined character. Now a man may be evil, but I believe that people can be evil in their essential natures and still have good characters. Good in the sense of being well-tuned. They can have characters which are flexible, supple, adaptable, principled in relation to their own good or their own evil — even an evil man can have principles — he can be true to his own evil, which is not always so easy, either. I think good style is a matter of rendering out of oneself all the cupidities, all the cripplings, all the velleities. And then I think one has to develop one's physical grace. Writers who are possessed of some physical grace may tend to write better than writers who are physically clumsy. It's my impression this is so. I don't know that I'd care to attempt to prove it.

MARCUS: Well, how would you describe your own style? I ask this question because certain critics have pointed to deficiencies in it, or what they think of as deficiencies. Didn't Diana Trilling, for instance, criticize certain flatnesses in your style?

MAILER: I think that flatness comes out of certain flatnesses in me. And in trying to overcome that flatness I may push too hard in the other direction. Alfred Kazin once said something very funny

17

about the way I write: "Mailer is as fond of his style as an Italian tenor is of his vocal cords."

MARCUS: Have you ever written to merely improve your writing, practiced your writing as an athlete would work out?

MAILER: No. I don't think it's a proper activity. That's too much like doing a setting-up exercise; any workout which does not involve a certain minimum of danger or responsibility does not improve the body — it just wears it out.

MARCUS: In writing your novels, has any particular formal problem given you trouble — let's say a problem of joining two parts of a narrative together, getting people from point A to point B.

MAILER: You mean like getting them out of a room? I think formal problems exist in inverse proportion to one's honesty. You get to the problem of getting someone out of the room when there's something false about the scene.

MARCUS: Do you do any research or special reading to prepare for writing a novel, or while you're writing a novel?

MAILER: Occasionally I have to look something up. But I'm always unhappy about that and mistrust the writing which comes out of it. I feel in a way that one's ignorance is part of one's creation, too. I don't know quite how to put it, but for instance if I, as a Jew, am writing about other Jews, and if my knowledge of Jewish culture is exceptionally spotty, as indeed it is, I am not so sure that that isn't an advantage in creating a modern American Jew. Because *his* knowledge of Jewish culture is also extremely spotty, and the way in which his personality is composed may be more in accordance with my ignorance than with a cultivated Jew's immersion in the culture. So in certain limited ways one's ignorance can help to buttress the validity of a novel.

MARCUS: Have you ever written about a situation of which you have had no personal experience or knowledge?

MAILER: I don't know. Let's see . . . *Barbary Shore*, for example, is the most imaginative of my novels. But I did live in a rooming house for a short period while I was writing *The Naked and the Dead*. I certainly didn't live in it the way Lovett lived in it. I never met an FBI agent, at least I had no sense of having met one at the time I was writing *Barbary Shore*. I am sure I have met a great many since. They didn't necessarily introduce themselves to me. I had never met an Old Bolshevik, either, although ironically, writing about FBI agents and Old Bolsheviks in *Barbary Shore*, the greatest single difficulty with the book was that my common sense thought it was impossible to have all these agents and impossible heroes congregating in a rooming house in Brooklyn Heights. Yet a couple of years later I was working in a studio on Fulton Street at the end of Brooklyn Heights, a studio I have had for some years. It was a fine old studio building and they're tearing it down now to make room for a twenty-story building which will look like a Kleenex box. At any rate, on the floor below me, worked one Colonel Rudolph Abel who was the most important spy for the Russians in this country for a period of about eight or ten years, and I am sure we used to be in the elevator together many times. I think he literally had the room beneath me. I have always been overcome with that. It made me decide there's no clear boundary between experience and imagination. Who knows what glimpses of reality we pick up unconsciously, telepathically.

MARCUS: To what extent are your characters modeled on real people?

MAILER: I think half of them might have a point of departure from somebody real. Up to now I've not liked writing about people who are close to me, because they're too difficult to do. Their private reality obviously interferes with the reality one is trying to create. They become alive not as creatures in your imagination but as actors in your life. And so they seem real while you work but you're not working *their* reality into your book. For example it's not a good idea to try to put your wife into a novel. Not your latest wife, anyway. In practice I prefer to draw a character from someone I hardly know.

MARCUS: Can you describe how you turn a real person into a fictional one?

MAILER: I try to put the model in situations which have very little to do with his real situations in life. Very quickly the model disappears. His private reality can't hold up. For instance, I might take somebody who is a professional football player, a man let's say whom I know slightly, and make him a movie star. In a transposition of this sort, everything which relates particularly to the professional football player quickly disappears, and what is left, curiously, is what is *exportable* in his character. But this process while interesting in the early stages is not as exciting as the more creative act of allowing your characters to grow once they're separated from the model. It's when they become almost as complex as one's own personality that the fine excitement begins. Because then they are not really characters any longer — they're beings, which is a distinction I like to make. A character is someone you can grasp as a whole, you can have a clear idea of him, but a being is someone whose nature keeps shifting. Like a character of Forster's. In *The Deer Park* Lulu Myers is a being rather than a character. If you study her closely you will see that she is a different person in every scene. Just a little different. I don't know whether initially I did this by accident or purposefully, but at a certain point I made the conscious decision *not* to try to straighten her out, she seemed right in her changeableness.

MARCUS: Is Marion Faye a character or a . . .

MAILER: No, he's a being. Everybody in *The Deer Park* is a being except the minor characters like Herman Teppis.

MARCUS: How did Marion Faye emerge?

MAILER: The book needed something which wasn't in the first draft, some sort of evil genius. One felt a dark pressure there in the inner horizon of the book. But even as I say this I know it's not true to the grain of my writing experience. I violate that experience by talking in these terms. I am not sure it's possible to describe the experience of novel-writing authentically. It may be that it is not an experience.

MARCUS: What is it, then?

MAILER: It may be more like a relation, if you will — a continuing relation between a man and his wife. You can't necessarily speak of that as an experience because it may consist of several experiences which are braided together; or it may consist of many experiences which are all more or less similar, or indeed it may consist of two kinds of experiences which are antagonistic to one another. Throughout all of this I've spoken of characters *emerging*. Quite often they don't emerge; they fail to emerge. And what one's left with is the dull compromise which derives from two kinds of experiences warring with one another within oneself. A character who should have been brilliant is dull. Or even if a character does prove to be first-rate, it's possible you should have done twice as much with him, three times as much.

MARCUS: You speak of characters as emerging, and I gather by that that you mean emerging from yourself and emerging from your idea?

MAILER: They are also emerging from the book. A book takes on its own life in the writing. It has its laws, it becomes a creature to you after a while. One feels a bit like a master who's got a fine animal. Very often I'll feel a certain shame for what I've done with a novel. I won't say it's the novel that's bad; I'll say it's I who was bad. Almost as if the novel did not really belong to me, as if it was something raised by me like a child. I know what's potentially beautiful in my novel, you see. Very often after I've done the novel I realize that that beauty which I recognize in it is not going to be recognized by the reader. I didn't succeed in bringing it out. It's very odd — it's as though I had let the novel down, owed it a duty which I didn't fulfill.

MARCUS: Would you say that there was any secret or hidden pattern being worked out in your novels?

MAILER: I will say one thing, which is that I have some obsession with how God exists. Is He an essential god or an existential god; is He all-powerful or is He, too, an embattled existential creature who may succeed or fail in His vision? I think this theme may become more apparent as the novels go on.

MARCUS: When did this obsession begin?

MAILER: I think it began to show itself while I was doing the last draft of *The Deer Park*. Then it continued to grow as a private theme during all the years I was smoking marijuana.

MARCUS: You have spoken so often of the existential view. What reading or individuals brought you to this?

MAILER: The experience came first. One's condition on marijuana is always existential. One can feel the importance of each moment and how it is changing one. One feels one's being, one becomes aware of the enormous apparatus of nothingness — the hum of a hi-fi set, the emptiness of a pointless interruption, one becomes aware of the war between each of us, how the nothingness in each of us seeks to attack the being of others, how our being in turn is attacked by the nothingness in others. I'm not speaking now of violence or the active conflict between one being and another. That still belongs to drama. But the war between being and nothingness is the underlying illness of the twentieth century. Boredom slays more of existence than war.

MARCUS: Then you didn't come to existentialism as a result of some literary influence?

MAILER: No. I'd hardly read anything by Sartre at this time, and nothing by Heidegger. I've read a bit since, and have to admire their formidable powers, but I suspect they are no closer to the buried continent of existentialism than were medieval cartographers near to a useful map of the world. The new continent which shows on our psychic maps as intimations of eternity is still to be discovered.

MARCUS: What do you feel about the other kinds of writing you have done and are doing. How do they stand in relation to your work as a novelist?

MAILER: The essays?

MARCUS: Yes: journalism, essays.

MAILER: Well, you know, there was a time when I wanted very much to belong to the literary world. I wanted to be respected the way someone like Katherine Anne Porter used to be respected.

MARCUS: How do you think she was respected?

MAILER: The way a cardinal is respected — weak people get to their knees when the cardinal goes by.

MARCUS: As a master of the craft, do you mean?

MAILER: As a master of the craft, yes. Her name is invoked in an argument. "Well, Katherine Anne Porter would not do it *that* way." But by now I'm a bit cynical about craft. I think there's a natural mystique in the novel which is more important than craft. One is trying, after all, to capture reality, and that is extraordinarily and exceptionally difficult. Craft is merely a series of way-stations. I think of craft as being like a St. Bernard dog with that little bottle of brandy under his neck. Whenever you get into *real* trouble the thing that can save you as a novelist is to have enough craft to be able to keep warm long enough to be rescued. Of course this is exactly what keeps good novelists from becoming great novelists. Robert Penn Warren might have written a major novel if he hadn't had just that little extra bit of craft to get him out of all the trouble in *All The King's Men*. If Penn Warren hadn't known anything about Elizabethan literature, the true Elizabethan in him might have emerged. I mean, he might have written a fantastic novel. As it was, he knew enough about craft to . . .

MARCUS: To use it as an escape hatch?

MAILER: Yes. And his plot degenerated into a slambang of exits and entrances, confrontations, tragedies, quick wails and woe. But he was really forcing an escape from the problem.

MARCUS: Which was?

MAILER: Oh, the terror of confronting a reality which might open into more and more anxiety and so present a deeper and deeper view of the abyss. Craft protects one from facing those endless expanding realities of deterioration and responsibility.

MARCUS: Deterioration in what sense?

MAILER: The terror, let's say, of being reborn as something much less noble or something much more ignoble. I think this sort of terror depresses us profoundly. Which may be why we throw up our enormous evasions — such as craft. Indeed, I think this adoration of craft, this specific respect for craft makes a church of literature for that vast number of writers who are somewhere on the spectrum between mediocrity and talent. But I think it's fatal for somebody who has a large ambition and a chance of becoming a great writer. I know for myself, if I am going to make this attempt — that the only way to do it is to keep in shape in a peculiar way.

MARCUS: Can you explain what you mean by that?

MAILER: It's hard to talk about. Harry Greb, for example, was a fighter who used to keep in shape. He was completely a fighter, the way one might wish to be completely a writer. He always did the things which were necessary to him as a fighter. Now, some of these things were extremely irrational, that is, extremely irrational from a prize-fight manager's point of view. That is, before he had a fight he would go to a brothel, and he would have two prostitutes, not one, taking the two of them into the same bed. And this apparently left him feeling like a wild animal. Don't ask me why. Perhaps he picked the two meanest whores in the joint and so absorbed into his system all the small, nasty, concentrated evils which had accumulated from carloads of men. Greb was known as the dirtiest fighter of his time. He didn't have much of a punch but he could spoil other fighters and punish them, he knew more dirty tricks than anyone around. This was one of his training methods and he did it over and over again until he died at a relatively early age of a heart attack on an operating table. I think he died before he was thirty-eight, or so. They operated on him, and bang, he went. Nothing could be done. But the point I make is that he stayed in training by the way he lived his life. The element which was paramount in it was to keep in shape. If he were drinking, you see, the point was to keep in shape *while* drinking. I'm being a touch imprecise about this . . .

MARCUS: Well . . . what?

MAILER: He would not drink just to release his tension. Rather, what went on was that there was tension in him which was insupportable, so he had to drink. But reasoning as a professional he felt that if he had to drink, he might as well use that too. In the sense that the actor uses everything which happens to him, so Greb as a fighter used everything which happened to him. As he drank he would notice the way his body moved. One of the best reasons one drinks is to become aware of the way your mind and body move.

MARCUS: Well, how do you keep in shape?

MAILER: Look, before we go on, I want to say a little more about craft. It is a grab-bag of procedures, tricks, lore, formal gymnastics, symbolic superstructures, methodology — in short. It's the compendium of what you've acquired from others. And since great writers communicate a vision of existence, one can't usually borrow their methods. The method is married to the vision. No, one acquires craft more from good writers and mediocre writers with a flair. Craft after all is what you can take out whole from their work. But keeping in shape is something else. For example, you can do journalism, and it can be terrible for your style. Or it can temper your style . . . in other words you can become a *better* writer by doing a lot of different kinds of writing. Or you can deteriorate. Craft is very little finally. But if you're continually worrying about whether you're growing or deteriorating as a man, whether your integrity is turning soft or firming itself, why then it's in that slow war, that slow rearguard battle you fight against diminishing talent that you stay in shape as a writer and have a consciousness. You develop a consciousness as you grow older which enables you to write about anything, in effect, and write about it well. That is, provided you keep your consciousness in shape and don't relax into the flabby styles of thought which surround one everywhere. The moment you borrow other writers' styles of thought, you need craft to shore up the walls. But if what you write is a reflection of your own consciousness, then even journalism can become interesting. One wouldn't want to spend one's life at it and I wouldn't want ever to be caught justifying journalism as a major activity (it's obviously less interesting than to write a novel), but it's better, I think, to see journalism as a venture of one's ability to keep in shape than to see it as an essential betrayal of the chalice of your literary art. Temples are for women.

MARCUS: Temples are for women?

MAILER: Temples are for women.

MARCUS: Well, Faulkner once said that nothing can injure a man's writing if he's a first-rate writer.

MAILER: Faulkner said more asinine things than any other major American writer. I can't remember a single interesting remark Faulkner ever made.

MARCUS: He once called Henry James a "nice old lady."

MAILER: Faulkner had a mean small Southern streak in him, and most of his pronunciamentos reflect that meanness. He's a great writer, but he's not at all interesting in most of his passing remarks.

MARCUS: Well, then, what can ruin a first-rate writer?

MAILER: Booze, pot, too much sex, too much failure in one's private life, too much attrition, too much recognition, too little recognition, frustration. Nearly everything in the scheme of things works to dull a first-rate talent. But the worst probably is cowardice — as one gets older, one becomes aware of one's cowardice, the desire to be bold which once was a joy gets heavy with caution and duty. And finally there's apathy. About the time it doesn't seem too important any more to be a great writer, you know you've slipped far enough to be doing your work now on the comeback trail.

MARCUS: Would you say that is where you are now?

MAILER: Let others say it. I don't know that I choose to. The hardest thing for a writer to decide is whether he's burned out or merely lying fallow. I was ready to think I was burned out before I even started *The Naked and the Dead.*

MARCUS: What kind of an audience do you keep in mind when you write?

MAILER: I suppose it's that audience which has no tradition by which to measure their experience but the intensity and clarity of their inner lives. That's the audience I'd like to be good enough to write for.

MARCUS: Do you feel under any obligation to them?

MAILER: Yes. I have a consciousness now which I think is of use to them. I've got to be able to get it out and do it well, to transmit it in such a way that their experience can rise to a higher level. It's exactly . . . I mean, one doesn't want one's children to make one's own mistakes. Let them make better mistakes, more exceptional mistakes.

MARCUS: What projects do you have for the future?

MAILER: I've got a very long novel I want to do. And beyond that I haven't looked. Some time ahead I'd like to be free of responsibilities so I could spend a year just taking on interesting assignments — cover the World Series, go to report a war. I can't do that now. I have a feeling I've got to come to grips with myself, with my talent, with what I've made of it and what I've spoiled of it. I've got to find out whether I really can write a large novel or not.

MARCUS: You once said that you wished to become consecutively more disruptive, more dangerous, and more powerful, and you felt this sentence was a description of your function as a novelist. I wonder if you still think that?

MAILER: I might take out "disruptive." It's an unhappy word to use. It implies a love of disruption for the sake of disruption. Actually, I have a fondness for order.

MARCUS: Do you enjoy writing, or is such a term irrelevant to your experience?

MAILER: Oh no. No, no. You set me thinking of something Jean Malaquais once said. He always had a terrible time writing. He once complained with great anguish about the unspeakable diffi- culties he was having with a novel. And I asked him, "Why do you do it? You can do many others things well. Why do you bother with it?" I really meant this. Because he suffered when writing like no one I know. He looked up in surprise and said, "Oh, but this is the only way one can ever find the truth. The only time I know that something is true is at the moment I dis- cover it in the act of writing." I think it's that. I think it's this mo- ment when one knows it's true. One may not have written it well enough for others to know, but you're in love with the truth when you discover it at the point of a pencil. That in and by itself is one of the few rare pleasures in life.

MARCUS: How do you feel when you aren't working?

MAILER: Edgy. I get into trouble. I would say I'm wasting my sub- stance completely when I'm not writing.

MARCUS: And to be writing . . . to be a writer?

MAILER: Well, at best you affect the consciousness of your time, and so indirectly you affect the history of the time which succeeds you. Of course, you need patience. It takes a long time for senti- ments to collect into an action and often they never do. Still it's no little matter to be a writer. There's that godawful *Time*-maga- zine world out there, and one can make raids on it. There are pal- aces and prisons to attack. One can even succeed now and again in blowing holes in the line of the world's communications. Some- times I feel as if there's a vast guerrilla war going on for the mind of man, communist against communist, capitalist against capitalist, artist against artist. And the stakes are huge. Will we spoil the best secrets of life or help to free a new kind of man? It's intoxicating to think of that. There's something rich waiting if one of us is brave enough and good enough to get there.

1963

Talking of Violence

An Interview with W. J. Weatherby

⚘

W. J. WEATHERBY: People use "violence" — like "love" — in so
many, often conflicting ways. Would you like to start by giving
your own definition?

NORMAN MAILER: Well, it seems to me there are two kinds of violence and they are altogether different. One is personal violence — an act of violence by man or woman against other men or
women. The second kind is social violence — concentration
camps, nuclear warfare. If one wants to carry the notion far
enough, there are subtler forms such as censorship, or excessively
organized piety, or charity drives. Social violence creates personal
violence as its antithesis. A juvenile delinquent is violent not because his parents were necessarily violent to him nor even because society is directly violent to him — he's not, let's say,
beaten in school — but because his spontaneous expressions are
cut off by institutional deadenings of his nature. The boy who
lives in a housing project is more likely to be violent than the
same boy living in a slum tenement because the housing project
puts him in direct contact with a deadening environment. The
housing project is not a neighborhood but a massive barracks.

Violence is directly proportional to the power to deaden one's
mood which is possessed by the environment. Threatened with
the extinction of our possibilities, we react with chronic rage.
Violence begins, you see, as the desire to fight one's way out of a
trap. Moral questions over the nature of one's violence come only

28

as a secondary matter. The first reaction, the heart of the violence, is the protection of the self. The second question, the moral question, is whether the self deserves to be protected, that is to say — was it honorable to fight? was the danger true? For example, if a boy beats up an old woman, he may be protecting himself by discharging a rage which would destroy his body if it were left to work on the cells, so he takes it out on the old woman. The boy may be anything from a brute to Raskolnikov. It requires an exquisite sense of context and a subtle gift as a moralist to decide these matters at times. Mexicans have a saying that when you commit murder, you carry the dead man's soul on your back, and you have to work not only for one soul then, but for two.

It does seem more or less self-evident that men who have lived a great deal with violence are usually gentler and more tolerant than men who abhor it. Boxers, bullfighters, a lot of combat soldiers, Hemingway heroes, in short, are almost always gentle men. It is not because they have read Hemingway. They were gentle long before Hemingway was born. It is just that Hemingway was the first writer who observed the repetition of this fact and paid his profound respects to it.

I think the reason is that men who are otherwise serious but ready for personal violence, are almost always religious. They have a deep sense of dread, responsibility, of woe, of reluctance to make an error in violence and a grim, almost tragic sense of how far violence can carry them. If I think of the athletes, criminals, prizefighters I have known, and the Negroes living in Harlem (their lives have much in common with precisely athletes, criminals, and prizefighters), they all have an understanding of life which is comprehensive and often tragic. It is of course deadeningly void of any kind of culture that could sustain them in their more boring times, but they do have a specific gravity and a depth of compassion which one doesn't find in their social opposite, the university-trained intellectual.

WEATHERBY: Is he protected too much from this kind of experience?

MAILER: It's not that he is protected from violence — although of course he is — so much as he is not in contact with existential experience, which is to say experience sufficiently unusual so that you don't know how it is going to turn out. You don't know whether you're going to be dead or alive at the end of it, wanted or rejected, cheered or derided. Now obviously there are few experiences which can by these rigorous terms be called existential.

But the hoodlum is more likely to encounter existential experience than the university man.

Something happens in an act of violence which is beyond one's measure. If a bully is beating up a friend who is smaller than himself and knows precisely the point at which he is going to quit, that's not really an act of violence. That's simply excretion. That's why we despise the bully. But when violence is larger than one's ability to dominate, it is existential and one is living in an instantaneous world of revelations. The saint and the psychopath share the same kind of experience. It is just that the saint has the mysterious virtue of being able to transcend this experience and the psychopath is broken or made murderous.

WEATHERBY: How does this view of violence relate to our own time?

MAILER: I wouldn't call the twentieth century a violent period so far as personal violence goes. It is a time of plague. When people sense pestilence is upon them, however, they *tend* to be violent. The powerful impulse of the twentieth century has been to defeat this tendency by elaborate social institutions which destroy the possibility of personal violence before it can have a free expression. If individual feelings are discouraged at every turn and social irritations are blanketed by benefits and welfare programs, then the desire to reach towards one's own individual feelings as a solution becomes stupefied.

The impulse of the twentieth century seems to be a desire to make society run on rails. Anything may be tolerated, even Communism, provided that the dialectic is squeezed out of our nature. The very materials of our world suffocate us everywhere. A perfect material example — the technological signature of the twentieth century — is plastics: materials without any grain, any organic substance, any natural color or predictability. Yet reasonable predictability, after all, is the armature on which great societies in the past have been built. Plastic, however, cracks in two for no reason whatsoever. It bears up under killing punishments and then suddenly explodes in the night. A fiberglass hull can go through storms which would spring a leak in a wooden hull. Then, one day, in a modest squall, the fiberglass splits completely. Or abruptly capsizes. That is because it is a material which is not even divorced from nature but indeed has not ever been a part of nature. Plastic is the perfect metaphor for twentieth-century man and for the curious stupefying bewildering nature of much modern violence.

Our obsession with violence comes, I think, not because its daily incidence is so high but because we are suffocated and so think constantly of violence. Can one argue seriously that our streets are less safe to walk on than the streets of Paris in 1300? Or Naples in 1644? But the twentieth century, in destroying a romantic view of existence, has created an awareness of violence as electric as paranoia.

WEATHERBY: Does this apply in the arts, too?

MAILER: There was a time when an artist could feel respectable about being a naturalist. Zola, Ibsen, Shaw were heroes. So were De Maupassant, Dreiser, Farrell. The natural work of a good artist is to try to write or discover what it is all about. Realism was a way of moving into this mystery just as manners was a way. Now, violence appeals to the artist because it is the least tangible, the least explored frontier. It's exceptionally difficult to write about.

WEATHERBY: Because it so easily becomes melodrama?

MAILER: It is difficult to write about violence because — like love — while you are experiencing it, you can't observe it. You lose your professional consciousness. Heisenberg's principle of uncertainty is in the wings: If you observe an action, the action is affected by the observation. Now, perhaps such emotions as love can be recorded truly — one's memory returns the truth. One can remember in entirety meeting a woman whom one was once in love with, and so be able to write about it. A number of sentimental memories can be recorded truly. An act of violence, however, cannot be recorded truly because the action did not create a mood but shattered a series of moods. So to write about violence is always an act of creation. One must make up an act of violence in order to write about it.

The marvelous thing Hemingway did at his best was to show that the only way to begin to write about half the important matters on earth was to create the mood or the destruction of mood in which they occurred rather than try to establish the truth of the event. It is possible that his years as a reporter inspired him with a passion for such emotional accuracy since he knew that the onerous duty of a journalist is to replace the mood by the fact and so create one kind of history, a fictional history, in opposition to the violent — that is, palpable — actuality of the event.

1964

Vices

An Interview with Paul Carroll, from Playboy

❧

PLAYBOY: We're reminded of your sentence in *The Deer Park* about growth: "There was that law of life, so cruel and so just, that one must grow or else pay more for remaining the same." Yet you've been charged by many critics with dissipating the potential growth of a major talent in American fiction by wearing so many hats. They point out that there's Mailer the politician; there's Mailer the journalist, who writes about the maladies in American life and about the political brutalities; there's Mailer the celebrity, who grabs headlines by booze brawls and other acts of public violence. How do you answer that criticism?

NORMAN MAILER: Moving from one activity to another makes sense if you do it with a hint of wit or a touch of grace — which I don't say I've always done; far from it — but I think moving from one activity to another can give momentum. If you do it well, you can increase the energy you bring to the next piece of work.

I've been accused of having frittered many talents away, of having taken on too many activities, of having worked too self-consciously at being a celebrity, of having performed at the edges and, indeed, at the center of my own public legend. And, of course, like any criminal. I'm my own best lawyer; the day I'm not will be a sad day. The defense I'll enter today depends on my favorite notion: that an expert, by definition, is opposed to growth. Why? Because an expert is a man who works forward in one direction until he reaches that point where he has to use all

32

his energy to maintain his advance; he cannot allow himself to look in other directions. In other words, he's become nearsighted. Now, I, as a man who's been nearsighted almost all of his life, know that anyone who's born nearsighted or becomes nearsighted early is a man become an expert prematurely. That's why kids with glasses are usually disliked by kids who don't wear glasses. The kids with good eyesight sense that the boy with glasses is an expert who's going to run the world. The first chronic personal shame I suppose I ever felt was having to wear glasses. And I don't wear them today, even though I'm so nearsighted I don't recognize old friends from ten feet away. Having been a premature expert myself, I think I may have reacted against it with a sense that expertise was the trap for me, that to get particularly good at any one thing would leave me top-heavy.

PLAYBOY: One of your celebrated experiments with growth was your experience with drugs. You were on marijuana, Benzedrine, and sleeping pills for a few years and were addicted to Seconal. Later, you said that a man on drugs will pay for it by "a gutted and burned-out nervous system." How do you feel about that topic today?

MAILER: Drugs are a spiritual form of gambling. This is a poetic equation that can be carried right down to the end of its metaphor, because on drugs you're even bucking the house percentage — which for a drug like marijuana is probably something like 30 or 40 percent.

PLAYBOY: Would you expand this?

MAILER: Marijuana does something with the sense of time: it accelerates you; it opens you to your unconscious. But it's as if you're calling on the reserves of the next three days. All the sweets, all the crystals, all the little decisions, all the unconscious work of the next three days — or, if the experience is deep, part of the next thirty days, or the next thirty years — is called forward. For a half hour or two hours — whatever is the high of the pot —you're *better* than you are normally and you get into situations you wouldn't get into normally, and generally more happens to you. You make love better, you talk better, you think better, you dig people better. The point is, you've got to get in pretty far, because you're using up three days in an hour — or whatever the particular ratio is for any particular person. So unless you come back with — let us say — seventy-two hours in one hour, you lose. Because you have to spend the next three or four days recovering. You might ask: What happens to the guy who smokes all the time? I don't know. But I do know something is being mortgaged; something is being drawn out of the future. If his own future has already been used up in one or another mysterious or sinister sense, then maybe the pot is drawing it out of the very substance of what I may as well confess I call God. I suspect God feeds drug addicts the way a healthy body feeds parasites.

PLAYBOY: How do you mean?

MAILER: Well, if God has great compassion, He may not be willing to cut the drug addict off from Him. During the time the addict has some of his most intense and divine experiences, it is because he is literally imbibing the very marrow and nutrient of existence. But since I do not believe that God is necessarily inexhaustible, the drug addict may end up by bleeding Him.

PLAYBOY: Do you think this happens on LSD?

MAILER: I don't think you have a mystical experience on chemicals without taking the risk of exploiting something in the creation. If you haven't paid the real wages of love or courage or abstention or discipline or sacrifice or wit in the eye of danger, then taking a psychedelic drug is living the life of a parasite; it's drawing on sweets you have not earned.

PLAYBOY: What is the danger of this parasitical self-exploitation on LSD?

MAILER: I'm not going to say that LSD is bad in every way for everyone, but I'm convinced it's bad if you keep taking it. Any drug is bad finally in the same way that being a confirmed gambler is bad. A confirmed gambler ends up losing all his friends because he blows their money and blows their trust. A gambler will tell any lie to get back into the action. By the same token, if you stay on any drug for too long, then you have a habit; you're a victim; to anticipate something, you're a totalitarian.

Let me put it this way: LSD is marvelous for experts to take when they get too frozen in their expertise. Let's suppose they've driven deep into something impenetrable, some obstacle that was bound to trap them because of the shortsighted nature of their expertise. Although they work and work manfully as experts, at this point they're similar to soldiers who have pushed far into enemy territory but are now up against a resistance they cannot get through. Their only action is to retreat, but they don't know how to, because they have no habits of retreat. They're experts; they know only how to move forward to amass more knowledge and put more concentration upon a point. When this concentration does not succeed in poking through the resistance of the problem, the expert is psychically in great trouble. He begins to live in increasing depression; he has to retreat and doesn't know how: he wasn't built to retreat.

My guess is: On LSD, you begin to die a little. That's why you get this extraordinary, even divine sense of revelation. Perhaps you taste the essence of your own death in the trip; in excess, it's a deadly poison, after all. Therefore, what's given to the expert is a broader vision: dying a little, he begins to retreat from his expertise and begins to rejoin his backward brothers. So that LSD taken a few times could be very good, I would imagine. But before very long, if the expert keeps taking LSD, he can become nothing but an expert on LSD.

PLAYBOY: What do you think of Timothy Leary?

MAILER: Well, I wonder who we were just talking about.

PLAYBOY: More of an answer, please.

MAILER: I never met him. Perhaps I'd like him if I did. Many of my friends like him. But I have heard him speak, and he is then naught but simple shit.

PLAYBOY: Alcohol seems to be another way by which you've tried to grow or "move forward." One of the characters in your stage version of *The Deer Park* declares: "A man must drink until he locates the truth." How does alcohol help a man do that?

MAILER: A man who drinks is attempting to dissolve an obsession.

PLAYBOY: What's the obsession?

MAILER: Talk first about what *an* obsession is. I've thought about obsession a great deal, but I'm not sure I know the answer. Everybody speaks of obsessions; nobody's ever really explained them. We can define them, but we don't really know what we're talking about. An obsession, I'd like to suggest, is not unlike a pole of magnetism, a psychic field of force. An obsession is created, I think, in the wake of some event that has altered our life profoundly, or perhaps we have passed through some relation with someone else that has altered our life drastically, yet we don't know whether we were changed for good or for bad; it's the most fundamental sort of event or relation. It has marked us, yet it's morally ambiguous.

PLAYBOY: What kind of event?

MAILER: Suppose a marriage breaks up. You don't know if it was finally your fault or your wife's fault. People move forward into the future out of the way they comprehend the past. When we don't understand our past, we are therefore crippled. Use the metaphor of the Army here: If you move forward to attack a town and the center of this attack depends upon a road that will feed your attack, and this road passes through a town, yet you don't know if your people hold it or someone else does, then obviously, if you were a general, you'd be pretty obsessive about that town. You'd keep asking, "Will you please find out who is there?" You'd send out reconnaissance parties to locate the town, enter it, patrol it. If all sorts of mysterious things occurred — if, for example, your reconnaissance platoon didn't return — you'd feel so uncertain you might not move forward to attack. The obsession is a search for a useful reality. What finally did occur? What is real?

PLAYBOY: You haven't told us yet how drink helps dissolve an obsession.

MAILER: Well, if a man's drink takes him back to an earlier, younger state of sensitivity, it is then taking him to a place back of the place where he originally got into the impasse that created the obsession. If you can return to a state just preceding the one you were in when these various ambiguous events occurred, you can say to yourself, "Now, I'm approaching the event again. What really did happen? Who was right? Who was wrong? Let me not miss it this time." A man must drink until he locates the truth. I think that's why it's so hard for people to give up booze. There's an artwork going on with most serious drinkers. Usually, it's a failed artwork. Once again, one's playing against the house percentage: one drinks, one wrecks one's liver, dims one's vision, burns out one's memory. Drinking is a serious activity — a serious moral and spiritual activity. We consume ourselves in order to search for a truth.

PLAYBOY: Do you feel that you've experienced moments of truth through drink?

MAILER: Extraordinary moments.

PLAYBOY: What sort of thing did you discover?

MAILER: Whatever the truth was. The kind of truths you find in moments like that. Discovering that somebody you thought loved you, hated you, or vice versa. All I'm underlining is that sense of certainty we all know when past moments of ambiguity are resolved. A relationship alters in one's memory from a morass to a crystal of recollection.

PLAYBOY: You've made in *An American Dream* and other writings a brilliant, dazzling, and rather puzzling remark concerning the possibility that God Himself may be involved in a process of growth. You've said that you have an "obsession with how God exists," and you've argued for the possibility that He may be a God whose final nature is not yet comprehended, even by Himself. Could you comment on this?

MAILER: I think I decided some time ago that if there is a God and He's all-powerful, then His relation to us is absurd. All we can see in our human condition are thundering, monumental disproportions, injustices of such dimension that even the conservative notion of existence — which might postulate that man is here on earth not to complain but to receive his just deserts and that the man who acts piggishly on earth will be repaid in hell, regardless of whether he was rich or poor — yes, even this conservative vision depends on a God who is able to run a world of reasonable proportions. If the only world we have is one of abysmal, idiotic disproportions, then it becomes too difficult to conceive of an all-powerful God who is all good. It is far easier to conceive of a God who died, or who is dying, or who is an imperfect God. But once I begin to think of an imperfect God, I can imagine a Being greater than ourselves, who nonetheless shares His instinctive logic with us. We as men seek to grow, so He seeks to grow. Even as we each have a conception of being — my idea of how we should live may triumph over yours, or yours over mine — so, in parallel, this God may be engaged in a similar war in the universe with other gods. We may even be the embodiment, the expression of His vision. If we fail, He fails, too. He is imperfect in the way we are imperfect. He is not always as brave or extraordinary or as graceful as He might care to be. This is my notion of God and growth. What gives me sustenance is that it enables me to love God, if you will bear these words, rather than hate Him, because I can see Him as someone who is like other men and myself, except more noble, more tortured, more desirous of a good that He wishes to receive and give to others — a torturous ethical activity at which He may fail. Man's condition is, then, by this logic, epic or tragic — for the outcome is unknown. It is not written.

PLAYBOY: Could you talk a bit more about the relationship between a man and this God who is still involved in discovering His own nature?

MAILER: In capsule: There are times when He has to exploit us; there are times when we have to exploit Him; there are times when He has to drive us beyond our own natural depth because He needs us — those of us, at least, who are working for Him: We have yet to talk of the Devil.

PLAYBOY: You said recently that maybe the Devil is God in exile. What did you mean?

MAILER: I don't know if the Devil is finally an evil principle of God — a fallen angel, a prince of darkness, Lucifer — a creature of the first dimension engaged in a tragic, monumental war with God, or whether the Devil is a species of nonexistence, like plastic. By which I mean every single pervasive substance in the technological world that comes from artificial synthesis rather than from nature. Plastic surfaces have no resonance — no echo of nature. I don't know if plastic is a second principle of evil just as much opposed to the Devil as it is opposed to God — a visitor from a small planet, if you will. So when I talk about the Devil these days, I don't really know whether I'm talking about a corrupter of the soul or a deadening influence. I don't know who or where the enemy is. In fact, I don't have the remotest notion of who or what I'm working for. That's despair.

PLAYBOY: Existential is a term that crops up frequently in your writing: existential God, existential politician. In what way was Kennedy an existential politician?

MAILER: Kennedy was a man who could define himself — or, in other words, comprehend himself — only by his actions. He had such extraordinary ambition that if he had not succeeded in being President, he might have ended up a bad piece of work. There is such a thing as a man starting as a bad piece of work because he has a nature that is extraordinarily disharmonious; he lives with unendurable ambitions. If he succeeds in what the psychoanalysts call "acting it out" — with some scorn they say "acting out" — the fact remains that he also has to have huge courage, high wit, and vast imagination. Kennedy succeeded in getting to play the one role that could allow him to realize himself: the President of the United States. When I call him an existential politician, I mean that Kennedy had no nature other than the particular nature he discovered in himself by the act of living. If he had tried to live a more conventional life, he would have sealed his psyche in a vault and probably have died young and schizophrenic.

PLAYBOY: How do you feel about Johnson's Great Society?

MAILER: It's a comedy. The Great Society is not only not going to come into being but it shouldn't. It's artificial. Any time you find a great society developed from the top, what you've got, in effect, is a test-tube baby — artificial insemination of the worst sort. Let's say the Great Society is drug addiction on a huge political scale. It's similar to shooting B_{12} complex into your butt. The patient may feel healthier for a while, but the fact of the matter is that his ass has been violated. The flesh has been visited abruptly by a tubular needle that punctures skin, rips delicate strands of muscle, and cuts holes in a vein wall. To what end? The body doesn't understand. If you're in a fight and get hit, your body can usually understand that: it was probably mobilized for action. But what action are you mobilized for when a needle goes into your flesh? The same thing happens, I think, with economic growth.

Take housing projects. I see no reason to come in with these tremendous urban-renewal jobs that are unspeakably ugly and tear up neighborhoods; they are like metal plates put in your head or plastic tubes stuck in your gut. These projects disrupt a neighborhood. Instead, some of these tenements could be saved. You might have a scheme where a man could start by being given one hundred dollars' worth of materials — I use the figure arbitrarily — and a little professional labor, and he could set out to improve his apartment: plaster a wall, this or that; say his wife will be in on it. He's working for his own apartment. If he goes out and drinks up the money, all right, he drank it up and presumably he won't get anymore. His neighbors might lean on him. Not lean on him hard, probably, because if he's the guy who drank it up he's possibly the meanest guy in the house. Still, what you get this way is a house interested in itself; whereas the other way, housing projects, poverty programs, Great Society — any Negro who doesn't set out to exploit the white man who is giving him money is nothing but a fool. With such handouts, honor for the Negro becomes his ability to lie, cheat, and exploit the white man. Whereas a few thousand dollars given bit by bit to a man working very hard on his own apartment over a few years would obviously do much more for that apartment than twenty thousand dollars spent to renovate it by outside methods.

PLAYBOY: Prior to the riots in Newark and Detroit, you said that civil war would erupt soon in this country. Did you see it as happening between Negroes and whites?

MAILER: I think there's a tendency toward civil war — not a war in the sense of people shooting it out over the hills and on battle lines; but certain kinds of functions might cease to exist in this society — technological functions. It may be that people will lose the habit of depending on the subway to get to work, or people might lose the real possibility of driving into certain cities at certain hours of the day or night. What might happen would be scattered outbreaks of violence: people, for example, overturning cars in traffic jams. All sorts of things — products getting worse and worse, shoddiness at the center of production, breakdowns, fissures.

PLAYBOY: How much of this will be the result of what you've often and passionately condemned as our technological society?

MAILER: Oh, much of it. Most of it, perhaps. Another great part of the tendency toward violence might derive from our guilt of the past: we've never paid for the crimes of the past; now we're trying to bury them. That's one reason the technological society advances at such a great rate: it frees people from having to look back into the horrors of the past. Western man has never faced up to the slave trade, the colonization of the world, the imperialization of the world, the concentration camps — the list could go on as long as one's knowledge of history.

PLAYBOY: In *Cannibals and Christians*, you described the cold war as useless, brutal, and enervating. You said we should stop it and get on with the destiny of Western man. What is that destiny?

MAILER: A huge phrase — I suppose I meant that the West is built ultimately on one final assumption — that life is heroic. It's a Faustian notion. Of course, the West is also Christian, but there's always been a contradiction at the heart. Christianity, the gentlest of religious professions, is the most militant and warlike of religions, the most successful and Faustian of religions. Indeed, it conquered the world. In that limited sense, Christianity is the most heroic. The alternative to this heroic notion of man is the passive acceptance of the universe that characterizes Hindu or Oriental philosophy and religion.

One of the ironies of our century is that the technological society creates an atmosphere of such passivity in people that they are now prepared to entertain Oriental notions precisely because they have lost much of the real power to shape their own lives. The citizens of a technological society are as powerless as an Oriental peasant. Their living standard may be vastly superior, but their social impotence is similar: they command less and less; they are manipulated more and more. They may think they are picking their channel, but TV channels them.

The more we wage a religious war against Communism, the more we create the real social equivalent of Communism in America — which will be the total technological society. You can look forward into a future where Communism's technological society grows nearly identical with ours; the differences will be of

the mildest local color. For the natural tendency of the technological society is to try to clean up all sorts of social excesses and to
root out random oppression because these activities are illogical.
They interfere with the smooth working of the machine. You
never want a piston to drive with more force than is necessary to
direct the action of the machine; you never put a part in the machine that is heavier than it needs to be. So the natural desire of
the technological society is to create a smooth totalitarian society
free from the ranker forms of injustice. Its long-term tendency in
Russia is to make a totalitarian environment that is relatively civilized and pleasant. Both countries may well end by serving up a
life to their citizens about as anonymous and vitiated and pill-rid-
den and dull as some of our new office buildings.

PLAYBOY: Then why does America fight Communism?

MAILER: Because we're Faustian. We believe we have to grapple
with the universe; we have the secret faith that we are inspired by
a national genius that enables us to take on anything and do anything. The tragic irony is that in fighting Communism, we are
creating the absolute equivalent of Communism in this country.
And we will destroy our own Faustian dream in the act of fighting Communism, for the technological society looks to destroy
any idea of the heroic. Such ideas seem irrational and unscientific
to the technician.

On the other hand, each time Communism has captured some
small part of the West, it has been shaken by Western complexities that open huge rents in the Russian Communist ideology. A
backward country like Yugoslavia did more to halt Stalinism than
fifty military adventures dreamed up by John Foster Dulles. Yugoslavia introduced a complex notion into the center of Communism: the idea that there could be two kinds of Communism, each
equally devout and heroic in itself, each more or less oppressive.
This made the Communist bureaucrat begin to contemplate the
nature of his own system and therefore to doubt his faith and so
look for ways to ameliorate the oppressiveness of it.

Communism is cannibalistic, as I said earlier. Any ideology
that attempts to dominate all of existence has to split into sects
and segments, because the moment disagreement exists between
members, it cannot be adjudicated or compromised without
losing the primitive force of the ideology. Compromise impossible, splits occur. What you get then is two ideologies equally
monotonous, equally total, soon equally at war with each
other.

PLAYBOY: Opposed to this, then, is what you call the heroic destiny of the West?

MAILER: Let's say, an *exploration* into the heroic.

PLAYBOY: Is existential politics an exploration into the heroic?

MAILER: To a degree. Existential politics can be understood only by talking practically, specifically, about what you are going to do here in this particular place and time. After you talk about, say, twenty such situations, you get some notion of existential politics. Existential politics depends on a certain intimacy between the law and the people upon whom the law is enacted. For example, not that there should be no capital punishment, but that if someone is going to get killed by the state, then make a spectacle of the event. Let people watch while a professional executioner and the condemned man fight hand to hand in an arena. Since the executioner is professional, he wins practically every time; but he doesn't win to a certainty; that gives the prisoner some last chance to fight for his own existence. It gives him the right of any man to fight for existence under extraordinary circumstances. Such a spectacle also opens the public to the real nature of execution. Let them see that blood on the sand. They may then decide if they still want capital punishment. If they do, more power to them. They like blood. But at least one profound hypocrisy — our quarantine of the execution from the eyes of the public that decrees the act — won't be able to exist anymore.

PLAYBOY: You have any prognostications about the American political and social scene in general?

MAILER: I'm gloomy. The technological society sits upon us like an incubus. It's impossible, for instance, to have any contact with anything in your existence that is not incapsulated by this technological society. I can't take a pat of butter at breakfast that doesn't have some chemical additive to deaden the taste of the butter just a bit, and therefore my taste buds, and therefore deaden me, as well as line my stomach cells with a new if minuscule addition of the chemical. If you could eat a fresh piece of butter for breakfast, certain sensory messages might be able to reach down deep into the secret needs of your nerves — enough to enrich you. You might live a hint better. The technological society gets between us and existence in everything we do, the air we breathe, the buildings we live in with their abstract monotonous forms, the synthetic fibers we wear; ever notice how a rash from a synthetic fiber is more disagreeable than one from cotton or wool? The list is endless. I've written about little else for years.

PLAYBOY: What can be done about it?

MAILER: I don't know. My feeling is that there is going to be some extraordinary holocaust. Who knows? We may all die off in mysterious fashion. For instance, about the time we discover some cure for cancer, a new disease even worse will probably be spawned by the cure — just as new viruses were spawned in relation to penicillin. Modern disease and modern technology are inseparably connected.

PLAYBOY: You've often connected this, which you call "the plague," with the modern technological society. How did the plague begin?

MAILER: Jacques Ellul, in his book *The Technological Society,* suggests that the beginning of all scientific technique came from a perversion of primitive magic.

PLAYBOY: You've written that one aspect of totalitarianism is fear of orgasm, particularly by the liberal mentality, because the orgasm, you claim, is "the existential moment. Every lie we have told, every fear we have indulged, every aggression we have tamed," you say, "arises again at that instant to constrict the turns and possibilities of our becoming." Could you tell us more about that?

MAILER: Orgasm is the moment when you can't cheat life. If the orgasm was no good, something in you — or in your mate — was no good.

PLAYBOY: Do you still believe, as you wrote several years ago, that birth control is evil — that it's a kind of murder of what may have been a man's best son?

MAILER: Yes. In fact, not too long ago, I was reading a very generous review of *Cannibals and Christians* in a Catholic magazine called *The Critic;* and at one point the writer said, Of course, Mailer's ideas are almost absurdly sentimental about birth control. I am now to the right of the Catholic Church.

PLAYBOY: Indeed, the Catholic Church is presently struggling with its birth control position, in order to square it with the problems of the world population explosion and the individual moral problems raised by families that are too large.

MAILER: Regardless of what the Church finally decides, the problem of birth control is the same as all of the other problems in our technological society. They're all part of the same damn problem; something is insulating us away from our existence. My guess is that in primitive times it was more difficult to conceive and — as a result — more natural. In a just existence, the best things are always the most difficult. We notice that many animals don't conceive unless they really want it to take.

In our modern life, on the other hand, the body is so deadened at its sexual center by contraceptives and pills that we no longer can afford to be as selective as we used to be. This adds desperation. People now conceive too easily because they're afraid if they don't, they won't conceive at all.

PLAYBOY: What would happen if there were no birth control?

MAILER: It's possible that it might then become much more difficult to conceive, because there would be more real terror of conceiving for too little.

PLAYBOY: Isn't it also possible that the social consequences would be calamitous — if your theory didn't work?

MAILER: Perhaps — but one thing you can be sure of: People would start making love a lot less; they'd make it only when they really wanted to make it; they'd have to be carried away more. One thing I've learned in all these years is not to make love when you really don't feel it; there's probably nothing worse you can do to yourself than that.

PLAYBOY: The "technological society" more directly affects — and you would say, oppresses — the middle and upper classes. Is that the reason you've written that the lower classes enjoy a more satisfactory sex life?

MAILER: I think the lower classes probably have more sexual vitality than the upper classes. They tend to work more with their bodies than with their minds.

PLAYBOY: But according to Kinsey, the lower economic groups suffer from more sexual rigidity and engage in less sexual experimentation than the upper and middle classes.

MAILER: All such statistics show is the attitude to which people are ready to confess. I don't know how valid such findings are. What we're talking about here is old-fashioned sexual perversion. Members of the upper classes and the more prosperous middle classes tend to be fond of their own pet perversion; they look upon it as an entertainment, an adornment, an enrichment; the lower class, on the other hand, looks upon sexual perversion as weakness; they see it in its other aspect. Perversion has two aspects: it is an adornment; it is also a need, and so they see it as a weakness and they despise it. To the lower classes, need is weakness.

PLAYBOY: What do you mean by "perversion"?

MAILER: Whatever it might be — fellatio, cunnilingus, name it.

Lower-class people see it as a weakness in themselves if they desire it. Envision a strong guy who wants to go down on his girl. He thinks he's weak. Of course he's weak. Giving head to your woman is weakness; it's also a good way to get rid of some of your weakness. It's also dangerous because it gives the Devil introduction into the vagina.

PLAYBOY: The Devil? How so?

MAILER: Oh, the mind's a devil. Didn't you know? And connected to the tongue.

PLAYBOY: You've said that D. H. Lawrence was the first novelist who gave you the idea "that sex could have beauty." Do you continue to admire Lawrence?

MAILER: Lawrence is sentimental about sex. Sex is not only a divine and beautiful activity; it's also a murderous activity. People kill each other in bed. Some of the greatest crimes ever committed have been committed in bed. And no weapons were used.

PLAYBOY: About the art of fiction in general, do you agree with critics such as Norman Podhoretz who claim that the novel as an imaginative art is dead because of the recent incorporation of reportage techniques into fiction?

MAILER: Obviously, I don't. The novel has its own particular resource, which is magical. You can establish a communion between yourself and the reader that can be found in no other art. And this communion can continue for hours, weeks, years. When the novel is dead, then the technological society will be totally upon us. You'll need a score card to tell the Communists from the Texans.

PLAYBOY: Do you think you'll continue to write political and cultural essays?

MAILER: In a way, I've been working on one book most of my writing life. Certainly since *The Deer Park*, I've been working on one book.

PLAYBOY: What's the book about?

MAILER: Existentialism. That is to say, the feel of our human condition, which, by the logic of existentialism, is the truth of the human condition.

PLAYBOY: At the beginning of our talk, you said interviews sometimes serve as a psychic housecleaning for your current ideas. Do you feel you've accomplished that here?

MAILER: I hope we haven't had a curettage.

1967

On Science and Art

An Interview with David Young

☙

DAVID YOUNG: I am interested in your definition of what an artist is.

NORMAN MAILER: I'm not sure I know.

YOUNG: Let me give you a statement that stuck with me. Just one sentence. An artist is someone who perceives relations that are not noticed by other people.

MAILER: By such logic an inventor's an artist; a mathematician is an artist; a physicist is certainly an artist. Besides, there are great artists who don't see many new relations but have an exceptional sense of how various styles and manners work. . . . There are playwrights who don't have original plots.

YOUNG: Shakespeare.

MAILER: I think in one sense he's actually quite an inventor — the relations he discovered in language. His metaphors are extraordinary. You could work up a thesis that Moore and Wittgenstein are a reaction against the metaphorical concepts Shakespeare left in the language.

YOUNG: Let's go back to our first question.

MAILER: It's a riddle, talking about an artist. I feel as if I'm sliding around.

YOUNG: Maybe a definition of art might help. Have you ever read Martin Johnson's *Art and Scientific Thought*? He defined art as the communication of feeling. And science as the communication of measure. But how do you measure feeling? I don't think it's possible. Now you can measure an orgasm, I guess, by some means, cardiograph and encephalograph and all that kind of stuff, but I don't think that is giving you any truth of that particular experience. I have a feeling that art and science and myth and magic are tending to grow together as our thinking progresses in a general sense. I was particularly struck by this when I was discussing anti-matter with a scientist. He said the top twenty scientists who can really deal with this subject have had to invent their own language form in order to be able to discuss it, it's so far out. And it has been discovered that five thousand years ago in Tibet a very similar language form was developed by certain monks who were discussing the sciences. It seems like the magic has come full circle. To me art has always been — well, indigenous to magic in one sense or another.

MAILER: Yet we have so many artists who literally invade technology. It's getting to the point where if you go to the Guggenheim, three out of four new artists are in technology as much as art. Some of it looks as if an engineer took pages out of his workbook and stuck them on a wall. Of course, we can also say that the physicist invokes magic when he works. Oppenheimer has his famous remark about how he always knew he was on the trail of something good when the hair stood up on the back of his neck.

YOUNG: Robert Graves used that as a test for a poem.

MAILER: Yes. They're related. If you stop to analyze it, the equation sign is nothing but a statement of metaphor. When you say: "y equals x^2" you are in effect establishing a metaphor. Or, the obverse: Some kid in a gallery, looking at a painting, says "I see God in the yellow." All right, that's a metaphor which can be stated mathematically: The yellow in this painting is a function of God. A simple mathematical statement. Either way, artist or physicist has penetrated an equation into the substance of things. In that sense I'd say the physicist and the artist are closer to one another than the artist and the gallery owner, or the physicist and the engineer.

YOUNG: Right. They might be married in the older sense of alchemy.

MAILER: You could say that art and science only separated at that point where alchemy turned into science, and those who refused to go along with the controlled experiment were left with magic. And witchcraft.

YOUNG: That was when men dealing with the heavens split into separate camps of astrology and astronomy.

MAILER: Maybe the essential intent which separates the artist from the physicist is in their relation to theology. But I'd rather not use the word theology. Let's say, brutally speaking, it is in their relation to God.

YOUNG: You mean to their own notion of God?

MAILER: Obviously, they all have their own notion. If many of them can easily — physicists and artists alike — think of themselves as atheists, and I come along and say it hardly matters how they think of themselves, I still say the difference is in their relation to God; it is obviously a way of saying *I* believe in God. Obviously. Then, everything I try to comprehend in others is going to come out of this fundamental belief in me. That is, of course, an arrogance. But the only way I ever begin to comprehend anything is by indulging such a stance. I don't believe it's possible to approach a tricky or mysterious question without assuming that you're right, or at least have an hypothesis to carry you every step of the way — at least until you find out your're not right. Then you can begin to search for the error in your intuition. Other kinds of inquiry can only lead to the computer. There you put in your collected experience plus the reported experience of others and wait for a statistic.

YOUNG: No room for the intuitive leap.

MAILER: I would assume that while the physicist is titillated, even thrilled, by the experience of magic in his work, and while the artist is often drenched in statistical detail (since he has to deal with a world that grows more and more technical and difficult to comprehend), at bottom their interests are opposed and they're enemies. Because the physicist is finally trying to destroy the fundament of magic, and the artist is trying to blow up the base of technology. The artist believes (and this is the greatest generalization I can make) that all cosmic achievement is attainable within the human frame, that is, if we lead lives witty enough and skillful enough, bold enough and, finally, illumined enough, we can accomplish every communication, and make every vault within the cosmos that technology would attempt to make. In fact, we're not coming face to face with the fact that technology has probably come to the end of one of its limits. As we go off into space, we're up against the knowledge that even if technology keeps expanding at the same extraordinary rate, nothing seems to offer any possibility of getting out of the solar system for thousands of years. Which means we may have taken the wrong road. Somewhere five, ten, and twenty thousand years ago, man took the wrong road. He separated himself from those dire disciplines of magic which might have enabled him to communicate with the cosmos. In fact, this language of the Lamas that you were talking about might have been precisely that same language. They were dealing with matter and anti-matter; they were communicating.

YOUNG: I have a feeling that an artist pursuing that notion now may be what will save us.

MAILER: Well, I don't know if we can pursue it. I'm talking about savage sensibility. The sensibility of the primitive who requires it to exist. You see, the primitive obviously had senses which were closer to the animal. He also had fears closer to the animal. Those fears are intense. Anyone who has ever felt dread in any real way knows it's so unendurable an experience that one'll do almost anything to avoid it. So I would come near to arguing that civilization came out of man's terror at having to face dread as a daily condition. Therefore we created a civilization which would insulate us from the exorbitant demands of existence. I'm not speaking now of those smaller or unbelievably pressing demands in that time of growing or killing enough food to be able to live simply. I'm talking of that greater terror when the trees spoke to one, and the message of the trees was not agreeable, and worst of all the trees were right. The message one got from the trees was true. The storm they told you about — that terrible storm which was going to make the river wash over its banks and destroy your hamlet in three weeks was true. What a terror. What a terror. I'm saying that man did everything he could, you see, to get away from that kind of intimacy with nature, that foresight, that dread.

YOUNG: Do you think that the invention of the devil might have come about from that phenomenon?

MAILER: Well, I'm not so convinced the devil is an invention.

YOUNG: Which brings me to one of my favorite quotes of Carl Jung: "The moment you remove the devil from society, you only allow him to re-appear in an infinite variety of anonymous forms."

MAILER: I would make an obeisance to that remark. A doctor inoculated my two-month-old daughter for diphtheria yesterday. He caught me at a weak moment. I argued with him feebly. They've found through experience that it's easier to inoculate kids at the age of two months than it is to inoculate them when they're four years old or five years old because the kids pass through the discomfort of the inoculation in a few hours when they're infants, and they're sick for a day or two later on. The larger argument that maybe people who get diphtheria should die of diphtheria can't begin to be ventured into. The doctor would have looked at my daughter and me through slant eyes. But what ate at me was that I had slipped my daughter into the technological chain of being. Chemicals stuck into her body at the age of two months. She was now going to be part of the chemical balance, imbalance, balance, imbalance, that all modern medicine consists of. She had gotten into that synthetic chain where chemicals which never grew out of the earth are installed into our bodies and we react to that in ways nobody understands. I think they keep giving us more chemicals to keep finding that balance that they've lost. As I was talking about it, I suddenly said, you know, they do to human beings what they wouldn't do to machines. And it's absolutely true that technology has more regard for the machine and fucks with it less than modern medicine plays with the human body. That's what I expect is the ubiquity of the devil. At the least, looking at it phenomenologically, there are powerful forces working to separate man's mind from his body. The intent of technology is to allow man to be a mind independent of all needs which keep the body within physical limitations. The fundamental notion of technology probably is that there is no wisdom of the body which the brain cannot relocate within itself. In other words, the disembodied brain is a superior piece of intelligence to the corporeal flesh-enclosed brain. As an expression of that, a lot of the functions of the brain having to do with habit are being taken over by the computer, with the terrible danger that about the time we lose the mental ability to do the intellectual tasks we are passing into the computer, we will be unable to spot errors in the computer. That is, we will be able to spot the errors but we won't be able to locate where they are and how they got there. Nobody will have the will, or the simple stamina, to trace out the circuits to see where the error got in. It'll be too boring, since we will have lost the habit of undertaking drudgery in mental work. Boredom will be as insupportable to the mind in such a future time as fire now is to the flesh.

YOUNG: I'd like to give you a quote. A friend of mine says, "Art is inarticulately certain, and science is articulately uncertain."

MAILER: I think that's true. But it doesn't help much, because next you have to get into fundamental philosophical questions like the relation of the articulate to existence. An existentialist could argue that because something is articulate, it does not by itself offer proof that it has any relation to being true. It may have a relationship to being — we usually assume it has a relation to being — but it may not. For example: The yellow matrix of the pyramidal doughnut probably has no relation to being.

YOUNG: Are you speaking of articulate in the sense of the word?

MAILER: The word as opposed to the feeling, to the unvoiced apprehension of things. Language may bear the same relation to man that technology bears to husbandry, or at least to any of the activities by which primitive man hewed out his existence. For instance, if I am a primitive, and alone in a forest, and live with all the terrors and agreeable forces of that forest, and walk with the principalities of the gods of that forest, terribly aware of the huge and ominous sense of pride in that giant oak which I believe is the center of the forest, well, then as I pass by its periphery I may have an exceptional sense of over how far a distance extends the hegemony of the oak. Think of that as equivalent to talking about the aura which surrounds a human. When we speak of charisma, we suggest that as you approach someone who possesses it, you can't get too near before you feel that you're entering some envelope of their presence. You can be three feet away from them, but something has changed in your own psyche. It's what people speak of usually as vibrations. At least one form of vibrations. Like entering a field of resonance which surrounds certain people who are highly charged.

YOUNG: Like an induction coil?

MAILER: Like a magnetic field. I think the primitive lived in a world in which all natural objects around him had these fields. Wherever one powerful psychic field met another, there was a mood. Where the presence of the oak met the presence of the field of tall grass, so there was a mood, and in that mood the savage walking through was aware that he was a third presence who was picking up some sense of events to come. Or picked up some sense of the past. One of the characteristics of most primitive languages, I suspect, is that their sense of past and future is different from ours. For instance, in classic Hebrew, there is no firm difference between past and future. In fact, there are merely two tenses, the present, and another tense which has to do with actions which occurred *either* in the past or in the future. Only a very simple shift is made in that verb form. If you want to talk about the past, you remark, "I left." If you wish to indicate "I will leave," you simply say, "And I left." My God, I spent years thinking about this. What a different sense of existence! Since primitive man keeps no records, the ability to distinguish between his memory of the past, and a dream, becomes next to impossible. Of course, primitive people also employ last night's dream as something which will give them intimations of the future. And, of course, it's possible the dream, far from being a wish fulfillment, is actually that instrument which enables us to anticipate those psychic problems we can or cannot afford to take on in the future. In other words, the anxiety system of the dream gives us clues as to how much intensity our nervous system can bear in different directions. That is why we re-play the experiences of the day before through the complications of the dream. We dramatize them in our imagination. We put ourselves in tense situations to see how much dread we can bear. Therefore the dream deals with the future as it is based on the experience of the past. Which means both past and future are part of the same psychic river. So it's as if the primitive Hebrew saw his experiences forming into two halves: two tenses, two modes of being — the sensuous-at-hand which was the present tense, and the sense of that other time which was not at hand.

YOUNG: That would tend to make the present of less importance, I would think. . . .

MAILER: I don't know. Particularly since primitive man was not abstracted in the way we are. His present, whatever it was, had to have an extraordinary difference from ours. He had to be immersed in it much more as he walked through the forest. Of course, I'm going along now on the not necessarily mystical notion that nature is an exquisite receiving and transmitting set. It's possible that one of the ways God would communicate with the earth and the earth communicated back with God, if you will, is that every tree and blade of grass is capable of sending transmissions. Because parenthetically we know nothing about radio. If you scratch a crystal, and lead the vibration out to any wire of a certain length, called an antenna, why then another wire of an appropriate length attached only to a crystal somewhere else can pick up your signal. That is the basic transaction of radio. We've put it through a million improvements. Amplified it unbelievably. Yet what more do we know about the inner nature of such communication? The assumption may not be unreasonable that other ways of communicating are equally good. One petal of a flower communicating to a bee, literally. Some of the messages we don't begin to perceive. And so, as I say, primitive man, moving through these fields, still able to communicate with these oaks, would have intimations beneath the level of language. At a certain point he knew in the way a plant knows or a tree knows that a storm was coming, or disaster was on the way, or the sun would be beneficent on the morrow.

YOUNG: Yes. And we've lost that. Almost completely.

MAILER: Well, let me say, we may have lost it at the moment language began. Here is the point: Once there is verbal language, then man has feedback. He no longer communicates to other men the way he once had a dialogue with the tree and the field. So long as he was communicating beneath the level of formal language, he had only to come back from the field and other men would see something in his presence which communicated his message. We just assume that primitives grunted at one another. We don't know. Primitive man may have had to do no more than move into the clearing or into the caves where others lived, and others knew his message. Since he was transmitting mood, others could decide whether he was true or false. But language, while it will often create mood, must as its first function interrupt mood, interpose itself against mood. Mood may be able to survive this insertion, but it is a different mood. The moment primitive man began to speak words to other primitive men — in other words, the moment the articulate was commenced — so the nature of man's reception of an experience larger than himself began to be altered profoundly. And something was lost. For in the grunt had been sounds from every corner of existence, while now, in the words, were oncoming abstractions of existence.

YOUNG: Which brings me, if I may interject, to the idea of art being inarticulately certain. I think what you've just said ...

MAILER: ... is an expansion of that remark. Yes. Art bears a relation to those intimations of the primitive. I know it's similar to the experience of every artist if I say that when I get an idea for a piece of work, I get it. There's an illumination in my head at that moment with which I don't have to argue. Trouble starts because you can't keep that incandescence, that illumination. And in fact, the reason it usually requires twenty or thirty years to make a good artist who's dependable as well as good is that it takes all those years to learn how to lose the moment and recover it, lose it and recover it, and learn how finally to be able to get it back each day in some tremendously diluted and warped and tortured form, but nonetheless, get it back. Enough so you can continue with your work. If you will, it's a function of the artist's relation to magic. It's his ceremony. For instance, you said a while ago that the artist now tries to return to magic. But I think the horror of it is that there's no one alive who can return us to anything. Our senses are so destroyed that we may be a light-year away from that primitive man. There may be no road back to him. None ever. We may not be able to begin to do — to comprehend where we lost the way, or where or how we can restore it. The artist may finally be merely some sort of extraordinary recorder of the failure.

YOUNG: I think the big problem for art today is to try to get back to the sense of creating a spell.

MAILER: Maybe you have brought us to the real separation between the artist and the physicist. Because the artist always seeks to create a spell. Today, of course, the artist is no primitive man, he's all but completely insulated from the senses primitive man had; and he usually acts as a mediator between magic and technology, between the world as instinct and scientific fact. But no matter how technologized the artist is in society, his central impulse is to create a spell equivalent to the spell the primitive felt when he passed the great oak and knew a message deeper than his comprehension of things was reaching him. It's possible the primitive felt something analogous to what we feel when we encounter a great work of art which tunes us in to some comprehension of something we can't even quite call any longer our knowledge. It's larger and less definable; to employ the word again, it's more resonant. It's as if art seeks to restore men and women by reproducing in them that sense of a lost spell, as if the artist is some sort of magician or midwife between the lost life of the primitive and the modern world of technology. And, if you will, the ultimate intent of the technologist, or any physicist who is drowned in technology one way and another, is to try to find ways of coping with existence which are independent of the spell. For the spell cannot be measured.

YOUNG: Do you think that art has much chance to flourish in this regard?

MAILER: Well, I think we've begun to come around some extraordinary corner. There is a recognition among technicians themselves that something desperately bad is happening in the very foundations of technology. That the whole machine of technology may

finally have been bolted to a base which will not remain perma-
nent, which is in fact rotting beneath. Sometimes, it's only when
man enters a series of failures which destroy belief in a huge endeavor that a huge endeavor in an opposite direction can begin.
The failure of the Crusades opened the Renaissance. I think this
is happening now. I think one note of hope we can feel in these
times is that faith in technology is beginning to waver, and in fact,
it's possible technology is going to go through a period as destruc-
tive to its ambitions as was technology to theology. We could advance the argument that theology was a species of spiritual technology designed to insulate man from existential existence, from
the lost senses of the primitive. Failing to work, theology was re-
placed by technology, but technology, in turn, if it fails to
work — well, at that point, it seems to me there is nothing left but
a return — if there's *anything* left — to the old notions of magic
which orbit around the fundamental notion that we are capable of
extraordinary psychic communication, not only with each other,
but with elements of the universe we haven't begun to conceive.
That may be the great turn of the wheel of history — that is, if we
can clear the ecological system of the world. We may not be able
to. We may be in the position of an invalid who's going to linger,
even for centuries, in some sort of half existence. That could also
happen. There's no reason to assume man was not capable of permanently injuring the world he inhabited. We may live on as
some sort of crippled social existence.

YOUNG: Waiting for the freeze bags.

MAILER: I wouldn't doubt it. It's the apathetic people, I'd guess,
who generate huge passions on the idea of a freeze bag. Technology sells people the notion they're going to give them something
for nothing. Which is the essence of the message of the Devil. The
reason the Devil is associated with magic in people's minds is that
magic implies it will give something for nothing. But the word
magic rather might suggest that there are subterranean relations
between things which are deeper than we recognize. But never
will you get something for nothing. Precisely, it's technology
which promises that something for nothing by sidestepping all
the disciplines of magic.

YOUNG: Perhaps it's this awareness of subterranean relations between things that does constitute a good part of what an artist is
today.

MAILER: Well, I expect an artist secretly assumes he has some fine
and subtle and possibly quite private relation to magic. In some

way, some little part of magic is his. He often pays for it by finding himself ineffectual and even tortured by the world. So it isn't
as if he's getting something for nothing with his magic. But it's as
if, if you will, that people who opt for magic are deciding that
they want a life which will have huge advantages and tremendous
disadvantages. They're stepping out of the sort of ordinary expectations other people have. Stepping into more and into less.

YOUNG: Choosing perhaps to be more alive.

MAILER: More alive and more bugged. More reduced. I mean, think
of people you've known who lived in depression for ten years at a
time — you think quickly of artists . . . Because of their sensitivity, their paranoia, because of their relation to magic . . . their
exquisite sensitivity to the possibilities of magic, to that communication between subterranean events which everything paranoid in one (for paranoia has to be a disturbed function of the
magical sense) would believe is having a powerful effect upon superficial everyday events. So when things are not breaking well,
such an artist will never get free of anxiety. His sense of magic
will keep producing more exotic conclusions. I mean, there's a
reason why man deserted magic and went into technology. Men
led lives of exacerbated uneasiness when they lived in the time of
primitive man and his magic. They sought, after all, to escape
primitive existence and existential life, in order to gain technological life. For precisely the reason that they thought it would be
easier. Now we've found that it isn't easier. It may even be
deadly. So now we've got to go back.

YOUNG: Would you see any relation to such going back in the way
hippies will wear their grandmother's clothes out of the attic or
just any kind of thing they feel like putting on? Is that sort of
stepping outside of fashion and in a sense stepping outside of
time?

MAILER: Oh, I think that's no mean nor small phenomenon. Maybe
it isn't so much stepping outside of time, as some profound desire
to reverse time. You see, hippies taking all those exceptional LSD
trips saw futures in man's continuation that were so terrifying
that they recoiled. That recoil has projected them back to the
nineteenth century. It's interesting that most of them do go for
nineteenth-century styles. You could say it's for practical reasons.
Nineteenth-century styles are easier to find, to copy, imitate and
wear, than eighteenth-century styles — But it's possible if this
continues that we will see all the centuries repeated, possible that

people in one era will yet be wearing all the clothes ever worn on earth. Yes, suppose we have got to go back to that universal dread we tried to escape five, ten, fifteen, twenty-five thousand years ago. Suppose it's now become the underlying trip of the world.

1970

In Search
of the Devil

An Interview with Richard Stratton

RICHARD STRATTON: Let's talk about psychopathy and murder. To what degree do you think Charles Manson might be an embodiment of some of the ideas you brought up originally in "The White Negro"? For some time I've been living with the unpopular thought that Manson was probably a very brave man in certain ways.

NORMAN MAILER: I think there's no question he was brave. One of the more depressing manifestations of public morality is that whenever someone commits a horror or monstrosity, they have to call the criminal a coward. It's automatic. Hitler's a coward. We used to call Tito a coward. Now they call Manson a coward. Part of the pain of maturity is that you come to recognize bravery is not enough. First you break out of the barbed-wire cocoon of a middle-class life with the idea that bravery is crucial to your existence. Maybe it's because the need for bravery is the one thing the middle class has refused to teach. So there's a period in one's life where you believe that anyone who does something brave is good.

Hemingway never got over that discovery. He had a cushioned life until he broke out of it, and like all of us he never broke out of it altogether. Then, years later, you come face to face with the

"In Search of the Devil" excerpted from "The Rolling Stone Interview with Norman Mailer" by Richard Stratton from *Rolling Stone* No. 177, January 2, 1975 and No. 178, January 16, 1975. By Straight Arrow Publishers, Inc. © 1975. All rights reserved. Reprinted by permission.

second recognition that people can be brave and still be no fucking good. That some brave people can be worse than cowards, and you can rue the day they discovered the grace of their own bravery, because finally they destroy even more than cowards do. Then you're face to face with the complexity of things and the difficulty of finding your way to any coherent ethics.

Manson is one of the most perfect examples of this. Because whatever else he is, you can't take away from him the fact that he's a brave man. Now, he wasn't altogether a brave man. And he wasn't a warrior. I mean, finally he was a general who sent his troops out to wreak the carnage, and he stayed behind.

STRATTON: But there were apparently certain aspects of his own personality which were very brave.

MAILER: Well, as an intellectual he was brave.

STRATTON: Yes. Then there was his method of dealing with men who tried to give him trouble. He was known to offer the weapon to the person he was fighting with and say, "Go ahead and kill me." And if that person didn't have the nerve to kill him, which . . . they didn't . . .

MAILER: Who ever has the nerve then? It's very hard to kill someone who stands before you, looks into your eyes and says, kill me.

STRATTON: That's bravery, and an instinctual sense of your opponent's strength, because no one ever took him up on the challenge.

MAILER: Well, that's not bravery, I'd say. That's a knowledge of the con, which is something else. Manson did grow up in prisons. He certainly understood that when you get into trouble you can't handle, then you still have the option to stand there and let the other person get their executioner's desire up to the point where they're going to kill you. It's not automatic.

It's reputed that Jimmy Hoffa once said: Flee a knife, and charge a gun. I have no idea if he ever said it, but I think, if he didn't, somebody who knew an awful lot about the subject had to be the author. Because there is something intimate about a knife, whereas there's something closer to moral decision about a gun. If you charge the gun, the man who holds it finally has to say to himself (since it's not a physical act, but a mental act), has to say to himself that he has the right to shoot you. At that point his moral sense of himself has to be invoked. He may not feel the sanction to shoot. Whereas if you charge a man who has a knife, his physical sense of himself is invoked, it's competitive. Am I going to hold this knife while he gets it away from me and humiliates me? But if you take your own knife and hand it over to the other man, that's different from charging a man with a knife.

We go back to the original advice: Flee a knife, charge a gun. If you hand it over and say, "Stab me," you make the knife a gun. And Manson may have had a particularly shrewd sense that the guy he was handing the knife to was a gun man. Weapons are metaphors which fit or do not fit our lifestyle. We do not mix metaphors when it comes to execution. So what we know about Manson is that he wasn't necessarily so brave about these matters as extraordinarily intelligent.

STRATTON: And he had an uncanny sense of where each personality he came in contact with was coming from.

MAILER: Oh, by every report he had an incredible sense of the people he was among. Obviously he had one of the more incandescent sensibilities of our time. The horror of it — not the horror so much as the pathetic aspect of it — is that once again we have a prisoner who's filled with talent, you know, the criminal who leads a prison life from beginning to end. Like Genet. Extraordinary talents. If Manson had become an intellectual, he would have been most interesting. He had bold ideas, and he carried them out — he worked for his ideas. The thing that characterizes Manson's life, whenever you look at it, is how hard that man worked for his ideas.

I like his sense of all these junior debutantes that would get into his gang. He'd have them out there, rolling in what? — not human shit, not cow shit — horse shit. Because if there's any single point of focus of social life in the upper middle class of America, it's that a young lady learns to ride a horse well and live comfortably with horse shit. Which of course is, you know, vastly more compatible than human shit or cow shit or dog shit or, perish the mark, wipe us out, cat shit. So, you know, there he has them rolling in horse shit. He knows how to get an orgy going.

STRATTON: Remember the day you and I went out to see the Spahn Ranch and found it had been bulldozed into nonexistence, which seems to me strikingly American. Like our attitude toward death, cover it up, make believe it doesn't really exist.

MAILER: Well, it's the American way. You know, we must destroy the past. When I was down in Dallas many years ago, a couple of years after Jack Kennedy was assassinated, naturally what's the first thing I do, I went over to see the plaza — the second thing: I went to see what happened to Jack Ruby's burlesque club. And you know, it had become a police gymnasium. They know how to do things in Dallas.

STRATTON: They know how to cut a connection or two.

MAILER: Right on.

STRATTON: To what degree do you think Manson was psychopathic? He had that other side to his personality, that hustler/pimp workingman's aspect. All the time he was doing his supposedly messianic trip with these young people, he was also hustling.

MAILER: Well, let's start playing with these words, set them up against each other. Not every psychopath is a hustler, not every hustler is a psychopath. Still, it's very hard to be a hustler without having some psychopath in you. It's hard to stay alive as a psychopath if you can't hustle a little. But we have to consider that at bottom the two are qualities opposed. Being a psychopath is existential. You don't know how a situation is going to turn out because you can't control it. Something inside you will not let you cut off the experience. You may be getting every warning that this experience is taking you into more and more bad places, and you can even get killed before the night's out.

STRATTON: Whereas the hustler tries to control the flow of the experience.

MAILER: The hustler's dignity is that he controls the flow of the experience. He considers it obscene if he doesn't.

Of course there's no such thing as a true or pure psychopath. Nor a total hustler. The hustler has elements in himself which are unmanageable, the psychopath has veins of shrewdness, calm judgment and a great ability to hustle. Part of the comedy in criminal affairs is to see how practical, sane, genteel, reasonable, clever and full of the final trick the hustler is. I mean, a good hustler always has a smooth hustle. Smooth's a word that fits with hustle. A player hates it if his cool is pricked. Manson is an intense mixture of the two. He's more psychopathic than just about any psychopath and more of a hustler than any average hustler that's come along. The vulgarity is to seize a personality as Dostoyevskian as Manson's and assume immediately that he has to be uniquely a hustler and everything he did was as a hustler, so don't take him seriously. Or else see him as an example of pure evil, unrestrained psychopathy.

STRATTON: That's always seemed to me the problem with Truman Capote's work. I mean, even in *In Cold Blood*, where he looks for those easy, quick psychological containers he can pour his characters into. I don't think he got any real insight into those two characters, the murderers in *In Cold Blood*.

MAILER: Well, Truman's abilities, I think, lie in another direction. Truman's always had an exquisite sense of his readership. Which I must say has changed greatly during his career. He started with a special readership. And moved out to an enormously large one. But he's always had this exceptional sense of how much they can bear. And he has always had the accompanying sense of how to vibrate their prejudices without shaking them apart.

STRATTON: And he knows how to end a book just beautifully, the way he ended *In Cold Blood* with that young lady visiting the grave of her murdered friend.

MAILER: Truman's never without his tone. And it would be part of his virtuosity that the elegiac tone would belong naturally to him. Yes. It would be hard to think of Truman ending a book badly. The first time Truman does, I will have to sit down and read that book all over again because it's possible that Truman will have just written far and away his most adventurous book.

STRATTON: Because he's on to something?

MAILER: The only reason Truman couldn't end a book fantastically well is because he would be on to something large. So, I agree with you about *In Cold Blood* in the sense that I don't think he got near his characters. I think that what he did do, which makes it an important book to me, is end up telling us more about the prejudices and the limited ability of the middle-class reader to encounter criminality than any book I ever read. It tells you almost nothing about the criminals, but how much it does say about that sense of everything-in-its-place that *The New Yorker* has stood for for over forty embattled years.

STRATTON: Perhaps Manson and people who can live with these extremities in their personalities may in fact be the survivors. And all the highly civilized people may be ending up in the worst kind of deaths to themselves. And technological destruction. If it's only in extremes that the society will save itself, then the secret fear of most people is that they're dead ... moribund ... and these Manson people are more alive than they are.

MAILER: Yes, I think that's what they do fear. And I think the reason is we have all grown up in a society that's relatively new in its fundamental premise, a society that claims to believe in life. To coin a piece of jargon, of the worst sort, we could say that we exist in a keep-everybody-alive society. Ironically, most of the cultures to exhibit great energy in history, the societies which produced our society, were, on the contrary, built on killing.

The idea common to all animals, and prehistoric and primitive man, even among civilized societies like the Greeks, the Romans, during the Middle Ages, and the Renaissance, the idea was still that if you didn't have enough right to live — in other words, if you were a drag upon the mood and the energy and the sustenance of other people — you were better off — Christ to the contrary — dead. These societies were kill societies. They got their neatness, their elegance, they got their style — out of killing.

But we are a society which says in effect, "Be sure you live. Life is our only gift. We're not going to get anything after this." The kill societies, to the contrary, were religious. They believed in the immanence of God, or a devil, or in demons. Primitive man spent his time placating demons in every tree. If a wind blew a sudden leaf past his face, he began to propitiate some spirit. They believed nothing was accidental. They were, in fact, more scientific than we are, for they believed that anything you can't explain is tremendously disturbing, whereas we prefer to ignore whatever we cannot dominate with our minds. We wipe out the artifacts of the past as if they have no curse.

Well, this notion, this keep-everybody-alive society — is a vulgar notion. There's nothing more livid, more cancer-provoking, than the face of a distorted liberal who shrieks at you, "You're talking about a human being!" They always italicize — *hu-min*. You're talking about a *life* that can be *lost*, they say. They're the same people who will turn around and absolutely insist upon destroying life, the same people who will soon leap with glee to forbid people to procreate, that is, about the time we decide there are definitely too many people on earth and we have to cut down the population or we won't survive, they will end by insisting that people be electrocuted for daring to conceive without a license.

Of course, today, they're still on the side of keep-everybody-alive. So the thought that someone might be so profoundly repulsive that everybody in their immediate neighborhood wants to let them die, is something they cannot tolerate. Nor can we for that matter. We're not as tough as we sound. We too live in this enormous supermarket of suburban guilt. Because we know we are all destroying the landscape with our homes and our highways. There's such a gassy, dead dull air over everything. Which we create. When you traveled, it used to be the only bad air you ever smelled was in a smoker on a train. Now that air is over everything.

Fresh air is the anomaly. We almost do not know what to do with it. Given this guilt we live in, we opt for keeping everybody alive because we know we're destroying everything. But that's also why we're, on the other hand, nihilistic. That's why we laugh every time a line or an idea or a disclosure cuts the feet off somebody. We all sit in this guilt that we don't necessarily deserve to live, and that maybe we ought to get back to the old idea of the kill society. So people like Manson just drive us up the tree. This guy's going out and doing it.

STRATTON: Another aspect of Manson that upset everybody was the sex orgies carried on by the "family." The real horror for the American middle class was to know Manson and his family were engaging in out-and-out sex orgies, exactly what so much of the middle class were doing themselves.

MAILER: I don't think the horror was in the idea of orgy itself. After all, one of the unspoken solutions to suburban life has been the orgy. There have probably been more organized balls among respectable people in the seventh and eighth decades of American life in this twentieth century than any other time, certainly in any other mass democratic society. I don't think there's been anything remotely approaching the incidence of systematized orgy we have here. People putting aside Friday night or Saturday night for their orgy, with their neighbors, their special neighbors.

But these orgies have always been, by every book report we have of them, always highly civilized, indeed the most highly civilized expression of sexual endeavor you can find. I mean, nobody at an orgy ever throws a punch. Suddenly America learns about this orgiastic life in Manson's gang that ends in mass murder. Anybody who's ever been in a civilized orgy knows that what you're left with, besides a few interesting memories to feed that part of your fantasy which still needs to be nourished, is a kind of buried bleak sense not so far from murder. I mean, I don't know that most people come out of an orgy full of love. No, a cold icelike feeling is more usually awakened. Most people sense the orgy has left them more murderous than when they started. Now, suddenly, Manson comes along with *his* orgies, and Boom, the murders do take place. Indeed, it's as if the murders were cooked to the boiling point by those orgies. Measure the shock then in the orgiastic suburbs.

STRATTON: Because Manson didn't come from their numbers. I

mean, he had been seventeen years out of thirty-five in prison. So he was a natural to take the orgy all the way to murder.

MAILER: Well, I don't think it was that automatic. He also had something inside him he couldn't control at all. His paranoid side, where he saw the blacks taking over the country. At a certain moment he was going to rise as some sort of gray eminence for the blacks and yet at the same time do his best to wipe them out. He had those huge plans to flee to the desert when the war was coming.

In the crudest psychoanalytical terms, his real connection was to his own timetable toward disaster. It was approaching very quickly. Because he was a man of Napoleonic ambition, he took this interior sense his body and his mind were providing him — the psyche secretly saying him, "Man, the climax is coming. You will not be able to keep your murderous impulses in hand more than another ten months, another ten days." That's why we shrink before any fanatic who comes up to us and says, "The end of the world is near."

STRATTON: Let's talk a bit more about the women's movement. I admit many of the women I find most exciting, most impressive, have tendencies toward women's liberation. But I don't think they understand what they call male chauvinism. I love women who have great character and spunk and are not content with being put in any simple category. But I fear the real thrust of this movement is to demean love and attraction between the sexes. A man who loves women is a pig. It's an antiromantic notion. It's sexual technology.

MAILER: Hey, Stratton, this isn't the way you were talking a year ago! I mean, the women are getting to you. They're getting to me and getting to you. Let's face it, they're winning their war.

STRATTON: You think so. They're winning their battle, perhaps. Meanwhile we're all losing our war. What women's liberation does is diminish sexuality.

MAILER: Well — I agree that the tendency is to diminish sexuality. I'm not pretending to know whether it's going to diminish sexuality for *all* time. But I think the immediate effect has been to take something out of it all. That's right in the need of the century. It's still a technological century and too much instinctive sex mucks up the machine.

There are two ways a technological society can weaken sex, through huge puritanism like the Russians, or you can do it through huge license — pornography, a sexual revolution, androgyny, gay lib, women's lib — huge license is even desirable to technology if it'll consume sexual energy and keep it at a low fucked-out level. I mean, what's the use of being able to make love to anyone, any man or any woman, if finally your incentive is taken away altogether? If the hunt is gone? The danger? The rebellion? The achievement? If you now ram it home to a woman and show her where she lives, what are you doing? Naught but revealing the secret boar in your asshole.

STRATTON: "My cunt is my chariot."

MAILER: Well, God bless them. You know, their cunt is their chariot. No one's ever going to be able to write about the way in which my generation grew up, you know, with this secret, profoundly sentimental adoration of the subtle superiority of women to ourselves. That marvelous sense of a woman's wit, that sly sense of the point which arrived so naturally into their thought. That sense of audience a woman provides. That notion we had of ourselves as audience to a woman. That tenderness. That respect for the immanence of a mystery so intimate, so nice, so near, so funny. We were so much stronger than women, and yet not at all. They were so much more powerful than we were, and yet never at all — never in any way. We lived as such romantic and sentimental equals.

Now we've come into another world where we recognize that they lied, they cheated, they worked overtime to give us this lovely sustaining notion, but all the while their egos were being rotted, their guts were filled with caustic, they were left with the dishes, they were left with the diapers. Left with the pale smell of water and grease and the slightly more unfortunate smell of formula milk and baby shit. And saw their careers going down into dull, somewhat incomprehensible dialogues with plumbers. While we came back and bayed at the moon, and said, you do not support me sufficiently, woman, to enable me to reach the moon. You know?

And then a couple of guys reach the moon, and some guys after them, and they all talk like women libertarians when they get there. In jargon. In a total, perfect, hermetic language. We'd looked upon these men in awe. These guys were cats, they were going out and doing things that really would stop up our stomach. And they had done it, they did it.

STRATTON: Yet they were sexless.

MAILER: They weren't sexless. They were women's libbies. What no one will ever understand is, the first guys to reach the moon — they were men, you know, in terms of bravery. More man than I for sure, maybe more than you, Stratton. They were men. But they had the minds of women's libbies. They were working for the team. They thought of only one thing, can't betray the team, cannot allow an alien idea to ever enter their eyeball, their nose, their mouth, their ear or their fingertips long enough to disrupt the ideological system.

STRATTON: A romantic idea is an alien idea to them.

MAILER: I don't mean a romantic idea. I mean any idea that's not in the system. You could have an antiromantic idea, they still wouldn't let it enter. They have nothing against romance.

STRATTON: Women's liberation is ultimately a team effort?

MAILER: Women's liberation is an astronaut system.

STRATTON: All right, let's talk about the music we just heard. Truman Capote was hired by *Rolling Stone* to cover the Rolling Stones concert when they were here the last time to tour the States. And he finally didn't do the article because he said the Stones had no mystery for him. But there's a lot of mystery in Jagger's personality and in the personality of the group as a whole.

MAILER: There's something unsatisfying about Jagger. We must have listened to two hours of music. Jagger's always promising so much more than he delivers. You know, finally he's in a sinister bag — he is certainly of all, if we take the three, four, five, six major rock groups in the last ten years, he has been the one who was the most sinister. Yet he's finally not terrifying. Maybe that's what Capote meant, I don't know.

STRATTON: Jagger himself, or his music?

MAILER: His music. I don't know anything about him. I think that the Beatles, you know, can hit eight bars in *Sgt. Pepper* that are more frightening, even though they're not sinister. The Beatles had more of a sense of powers they could summon by playing the wrong note at a given moment. It's as if they're more terrified by music than Jagger. Jagger's terribly spoiled. There's all that muttering in the background: "Oh, no God, you won't break this heart of stone."* What a threat. Beyond that constant dirge, beyond the throatiness which makes you think he's riding on the rims, through all that electric masturbation, you know, all that sound of distant musketry, every drumbeat, there's still a mountain of bullshit. It's not getting in and saying, I'm going to kill

---

* "Heart of Stone" by Mick Jagger and Keith Richard. © 1965, Abkco Music Co.

you, motherfucker. It's not saying, I'm here to call upon Satan. It pretends to. Some of his music I find, you know, marvelously promising. But it's irritating as hell to listen to for two hours because you keep waiting for the great payoff, and it never comes.

But again there's a kind of bullying that I've always distrusted in rock. Which is, it doesn't take big balls to have a big electric guitar and a huge amplifying system and fifty thousand American corporations that they're all sneering at, working overtime to amplify them. You know, it's a little bit like some politician that you despise saying, I represent the people. He only represents his power in his microphone and his media, his vested electronic office.

STRATTON: But let's look at the Stones in context. The Stones have stayed at the top, they're still the most interesting group playing together. They're all good musicians. Even the Beatles, as musicians, with the possible exception of George Harrison, weren't very exciting. Ringo Starr could never compare with Charlie Watts for drumming ability.

MAILER: Their drummer's incredibly good. In fact, I think their drummer's half of them. Because you've got all that caterwauling, you've got all those half-heard threats, that sense of sullen curses always riding in the background, you've got that sense of disarray, sense of mama with her nerves broken looking for her fix. You got all that. But what keeps it all together is you got this great big driving beat. That you can make anything you want. You can dream up a Third World coming through, Africa rising. There's a — the tension of the music is that one world's dissolving into a kind of marvelous — I mean, their comic gifts are superb. You really get this feeling of androgynous family, and androgynous family relations, like maybe it's never been done. All that's first-rate. I'm criticizing them at, you know, what I consider the highest level. But finally at the highest level, they are fucking disappointing. They depend on noise. You know, we listened to them not at top high. At middle high. And they don't make it.

STRATTON: Take a song like "Sympathy for the Devil." You have to go a long way — Bob Dylan's probably the only other one, plus some songs from the Beatles — you have to go a long way before you get lines as interesting in rock music as, "Just as every cop is a criminal and all the sinners saints."*

MAILER: What's splendid, what's new about that? Dostoyevsky used to go into an epileptic fit he grew so bored with that notion.

* © 1968 Abkco Music Inc.

STRATTON: Well, there's nothing new about it, but compared to most rock lyrics, the Stones have at least considered Dostoyevsky.

MAILER: I don't think these lyrics compare to Dylan's. I don't think they even try to — I think, in fact, I'd almost go the other way. I'd say that Jagger's lyric is interminably repetitive in order to allow for that captivating tension between the guttiness in his voice and the whine. To play that back and forth, you don't really want too good a lyric. Dylan's voice is thinner. At times I find it nasal to the point where I can do without it. There's something a little boring about a man who comes from a fine Jewish family in Minneapolis sounding like an Oklahoma Okie.

You know, Dylan is . . . not Johnny Cash. So I find that part of it a little boring. Dylan's voice is much less exciting to me than his lyrics, his lyrics are superb. Selden Rodman was the first to say this, but I think Dylan may prove to be our greatest lyric poet of this period. Like many another lyric poet, he can't necessarily read his own lyrics. With Dylan, what I think you feel is that it's the poetry that carries the song, not the singer.

With Jagger, it's the reverse. Jagger has got this marvelous sense of the day in which a family breaks up. The son throws acid in the mother's face, the mother stomps the son's nuts in, and then the fat cousin comes and says, What is everybody fighting for, let's have dinner. And they sit down, the son has no nuts left, the mother's face is scarred, but they go on and, you know, British family life continues. Jagger's got that like no one else's ever had it. If he'd been a writer he would have been one of the best. But that marvelous quality isn't caught in the lyrics so much as in the ensemble of everything, sound, instruments, everything.

STRATTON: And his voice.

MAILER: His voice first.

STRATTON: I don't know if you can find another rock group capable of coming up with a song like "Sympathy for the Devil."

MAILER: "Sympathy for the Devil," I felt, was arch, and much too self-conscious. I couldn't quite catch the words and that's one of the things about Jagger that's always suspect to me. When you play on the edge of the articulation of words it's because you're trying to do two things at once. I did hear him at one point wailing about the Russian Revolution — that the Devil was there at the planning of the Russian Revolution and, you know, that's news. No good Christian ever thought of that before. That, I thought, was finally on the edge of the revolting. You don't, you know, you don't infuse a bunch of dumb, spaced-out, highly sexed working-class kids with a little historical culture while you're singing. Come on! I decided Jagger must have picked up a magazine article about the Russian Revolution the day before he wrote the words. But, you know, there's more profundity in "Eleanor Rigby" than there is in "Sympathy for the Devil."

I mean, there are a lot of vulgar plays in "Sympathy for the Devil," gay-aim for game. A lot of dull choices were made. I expected to be knocked down by "Sympathy for the Devil," and I wasn't. I think maybe it's historically significant. It may be the first song that invokes the Devil in I don't know when. You might have to go back to black masses in the Middle Ages to find a lyric that invokes the Devil. But that doesn't mean it's good any more than *The Exorcist* is. Which is to say, it's phenomenal as an index of the time. What impresses us is not how good the artist is, but that he's right at the place where people are going to react. So Jagger anticipated, just as Blatty did, that there's subterranean belief in the Devil about ready to emerge. Given any kind of encouragement, it comes charging through.

Which brings us to Satanism. The Satanism of shit at the highest level, the standard of Satan. It's his escutcheon. It's his flag. He says, You've been rejected, you've been wasted by the system, passed over, yet you are more redolent, more interesting, more sexy, more incredible, more funky, more filled with undeliverables that should have been delivered than anything they got going out there. And, for years, the Devil has fought a desperate uphill battle.

But by now, when we got those superhighways, with that gas, and the whole world's getting to look more and more like the Jersey flats, given modern life up front, the suburbs, the smell of the gas, smell of plastic in every home, carpets smell of the plastic and the kids grow up licking plastic, play with Play-Doh which has that smell between cheap perfume and deodorant; when you think of the prevalence not of death in every one of our phenomena but of the void — of the presence of void — in every aspect of successful life today, you travel first class on a plane which is an envelope presenting its concept of the void, get off that airplane into an airport which in turn presents its concept of the void or you go through a smog-filled superhighway to that city which looks like every other city — Moscow, I hear, looks like Washington entering its terminal cancer . . . you then go out for your pleasures which are not as brilliant as they were in the depths of the boredom of the Victorian period; there's no such thing as a thrill for anyone alive any longer. You take all this, all this degradation of the void; because we all move around with a profound sense of degradation these days and under it there's the Devil calling, saying I'm shit, I'm everything that you've wasted, I'm all that rich, crazy passionate fuck guck funky possibility, I'm that other culture. And of course there's a profound desire to move over to that.

Now, in this twentieth century where our senses, our souls, are being leached out, where we're all entering a void, the horror of modern life is that there is no horror. So we begin to wonder whether selling the soul to the Devil may not be a life-giving transaction. That's the underlying terror of modern life.

STRATTON: The Devil has always been associated with materialism. There was always, you know, the idea of the temptation of Christ with riches and the wealth of the world.

MAILER: That doesn't deny what I was saying.

STRATTON: So isn't it conceivable that what we might have done is, collectively, sold our souls to the Devil a long time ago; say in the beginning of the nineteenth century, before the Industrial Revolution?

MAILER: If we sold our soul to the Devil centuries ago in order to prosper materially, in this twentieth century we're not happy materially. We're not gorging like Romans. We are prospering electronically. And suffering materially in all the voids and stinks of plastic and pollution.

STRATTON: And lost our karma too, sold our karma along with our soul. We've sold our opportunity for transcendence. That's why we're terminal. You see what I mean? I think that if anything the Devil is winning. I think he's winning and I think he's gloating because he has more control at this point. I think he is the prince of this world.

MAILER: That's one idea I hold. What I pose against it immediately is that the Devil is also miserable, because finally the air conditioner is not the Devil's paradise.

STRATTON: True. But there are those other alternatives we may get into in the next twenty, thirty years, you know. That when people get sick of technology and air conditioners and all the sterile dead aspects of plastic, they're going to revert more and more to Satanism and to orgies, to bloodletting and to shit, all those things —

MAILER: All right. But ask yourself: All those things you're talking about, that you just named, are they equal to technology?

STRATTON: Are they equal to technology?

MAILER: Or are they the opposite?

STRATTON: The opposite.

MAILER: It seems to me you ought to have your Devil, just for the sake of this little matter, one place or the other.

STRATTON: Yes, I said that I think technology may be a tool of the Devil, a means to an end, the end being the complete leaching out of our souls.

MAILER: To drive people toward shit and blood. ·

STRATTON: Right. Right. This is Satan's cunning. In a technological and spiritually starved society, he may gain complete control.

MAILER: Well, let me think about that. And have a drink.

STRATTON: Okay. Just to continue with this idea, it may be that technology is a transitional stage as far as the Devil is concerned. I've got to believe God is more opposed to the dead spirit of technology than the Devil would be. I think that the Devil may have said to himself, Well, it looks to me like the only way I'm ever going to win final control over mankind is to offer them all those things they seem to want most, material comforts, wealth, prosperity and lack of suffering, to eliminate suffering from the world. People don't want to suffer, they immediately reach for a pill, mother's little helper.

So, my notion, anyway, is that technology, science, pollution, whatever, is finally probably a tool of the Devil that is going to starve and deaden the soul to such a degree that man will reach out for the funkiness, then for horror — back to Charlie Manson.

MAILER: I think you're passing over too much. To begin with, there's no reason to equate science and technology any more than we put art and bestsellerdom together. After all, there's no reason to assume a bestseller is a work of art at a lower level. That may be a legitimate way to characterize a bestseller, or the opposite may be true, that a bestseller is the precise opposite of art, and to the degree the work is a bestseller, it is meretricious.

STRATTON: Technology may be the opposite of science, then?

MAILER: Well, I think there's much reason to believe that it is. Science, for most of its history, was essentially a poetic endeavor. Every metaphor, if you stop to think about it, is an equation. If you say, "The sparrow is on the wing," that's a scientific remark, it's a way of saying that the center of essence in the sparrow is within the wing, the sparrow is *on* the wing. It's a way of saying that the sparrow exists in two manifestations at once, body and flight, just as light consists of waves and particles. The sparrow is on the wing. As you start to bear down on the language, you begin to feel the very vibrancy of the wing. The condition of being in two states at once. The sparrow is *on* the wing. You can fix on that point endlessly because it's a metaphor, an equation, a moment of balance. Originally, science had that quality, that its fundamental recognitions were, dare I say it? — poetic.

STRATTON: It was an art at that point?

MAILER: Absolutely an art. Technology is finally, I would suggest, a tradition, and a dull one. A statistical tradition. Technology derives from General Ulysses S. Grant, who said that if I bring enough men and enough ammunition to bear at one point on this line, and if I don't care how many troops of mine get killed, and I just keep pursuing this, if my ego is finally larger than any question that's presented to me, then I am obliged to triumph because I do not care. And he won.

Grant changed the nature of war. Before that, war always consisted of the obligation to win with a certain minimum of skill and grace. There was a code of war. Robert E. Lee subscribed to that code, he believed that you did not win battles at any price, that you didn't lose half your army to win a battle. Because at that point something dreadful would happen. Grant, having to contend with a miserable drafted army, people who did not want to fight the war — the Civil War as far as the North was concerned was not too unlike the war in Vietnam, in the sense that the troops had absolutely no desire to fight — Grant just kept putting in more and more bodies to blast their way through the noise.

Now that's technology. Technology does not really care what happens in the aftermath, it wishes to succeed on this point. It does not even need to have theory in order to proceed, let alone art. It will push its way through. It is an ego manifestation, and — all right. There's nothing in this that says it's therefore opposed to the notion of the Devil. The Devil may indeed be ego. But we have to draw back just enough to ask ourselves one further question, and it comes up to me as follows. Where is God in all this?

STRATTON: Well, God may be the loss of ego.

MAILER: No, no, no. Face into technology. What's God's relation to technology? Do you believe in God?

STRATTON: Yes.

MAILER: Do you believe God is not dead at all? Is very much alive?

STRATTON: Yes.

MAILER: God, I would take it, knowing you fairly well, is a principle of some judicious mixture of courage and love?

STRATTON: Right. Absolutely. And harmony, a certain kind of harmony, a physical harmony with life and one's place in life and in the cosmos that is opposed to technology.

God, as far as I'm concerned, is mystery, and anything opposed to mystery, that tries to answer out all the mystery of life, is anti-God. Technology wants to eradicate mystery. I think at this point if God exists, He exists as a revolutionary, He's got to be a violent and passionate spiritual revolutionary, because He's out of grace at this stage, very much out of grace.

MAILER: Not out of grace. Out of favor.

STRATTON: Out of favor.

MAILER: Out of favor of what? The universe . . .

STRATTON: No, with mankind, with technological man.

MAILER: We still separate here. Because I think we have to face the possibility that technology is a third force, come to us from the cosmos. That it may have very little to do with God and the Devil.

STRATTON: May be separate altogether?

MAILER: Virtually separate. To go back to one of my oldest and firmest ideas, what if the universe is finally a series of conceptions which are at war with one another? And what we think of as God is only one conception of this universe, out there, at war with other conceptions? What if technology is an invasion of this earth from without? Because technology gives us no evidence whatsoever of having any sympathy for the nature of our world, nothing to do with our desires for an earth on which we can dwell.

STRATTON: No, certainly not. Its aim would seem to be to make the planet uninhabitable in the name of making us all more comfortable. What is a higher standard of living if we are all dying?

MAILER: Well, if at that point — you see — at this point we're reduced to speculation. Either the Devil invited technology here or, what I find more interesting, God entered into a dread compact. At a certain point he decided that Satan had so invaded affairs on earth that God could never begin to lead man up and outward to the stars. So some compact had to be made with technology. Technology, that spirit come to visit us from afar. If we dare to personify our divinities, there's nothing extraordinary about such speculation. Evil often triumphs, because good makes a mediocre compact out of some dire necessity. Where we're far apart is, I don't believe in an omnipotent God. I believe in a God who's like us only more so. Who has a vision of existence of which we are very much a part. Because we will either fulfill that vision of existence, or we will fail God.

STRATTON: No, I can't agree. God is perfection. I don't actually believe in an omnipotent god as much as in a god whose nature is finally unknowable, as is perfection.

MAILER: The idea that the nature of God is unknowable, at this point, when the world's dying in the exudate of all its diseases, is a cop-out.

STRATTON: Not if you think of God in terms of a quality, a state of being toward which you're constantly trying to become closer, to get more in harmony with, as an ongoing struggle.

MAILER: You've been saying that you want to talk about drugs a little, and I think they're related to this question in a fashion. I think drugs bear the same relation to mysticism as technology to science.

We're coming to learn that most of the world's mystics, in one way or another, have or had their drug. The mystical societies most mystics have been revering for centuries did have, in one fashion or another, their drug ritual. So, it isn't so simple a matter as saying that if you take a drug then you're a technologist and not a scientist. It does mean that there is a use of drugs among mystics and mystical societies which was reverential, ceremonial, sacramental.

The use of drugs today, if we're going to employ an analogy, is again comparable to the war in Vietnam: If you have a great deal of money to spend and very few results to show, and if you can't find the enemy, well then, goddamnit, says Barry Goldwater, burn down the fucking foliage. Scorch those gooks, get them out of there. Denude the land and you will find what is there. That is what the allegedly best generation of our young are doing to their minds. They're saying, If I can't find the idea I was looking for yesterday, I am going to take twice as much tonight.

STRATTON: I'll take a thousand more mics of LSD and burn down the foliage of my mind.

MAILER: Burn down the foliage of my mind to find some of those ideas I can feel running around in there. It's a military operation, it's technological.

I don't think drugs are going to find God or the Devil. I think what they're going to create is the scorched earth of consumed karma. I believe, you know, that one has to be as reverential about drugs as about sex. The mark of an utter idiot, in my mind, is to find, let's say he's a man who falls passionately in love with a woman. He finds this divine cunt and he not only fucks the hell out of her but fucks the hell out of himself until his balls are as wet as gravel. You know, he is grinding his ass up over the stones to get in one more fuck for the ego. He's gone over. He is a gassed-out, farted-out goose. That is our drug addict. That's what the drug addict is doing to mysticism. If God is a rabbit, the drug addict is trying to kill that rabbit with a thousand flails.

In religious discussion, when we start to talk about this tripartite nature of the confusion, God, Devil and technology, and what is with whom, it may serve us to take one little look at cosmology today. One notion that the physicists presented to us about fifty years ago was the idea of the expanding universe. The galaxies were traveling outward. There's reason to decide that we live in a universe which expands and contracts. Curious, isn't it?

More than that, a universe in which stars expand and contract. Stars exhibit red light in their spectrum and blue — red lights as they expand, no surprise to any of us humans, and blue as they turn cold. As they contract more and more, they turn black. They become the essence of matter, become so compressed, so black, that a star which was once a million miles in diameter is now two miles in diameter, a mile in diameter. It becomes so compressed that finally it is the size of your thumbnail and weighs more than the sun. At least, that is what cosmological evidence and theory has brought certain physicists to thinking.

At that point, there's a gravitational mass so intense that it pulls in everything to it. It pulls in light. Einstein delivered the general theory of relativity, which was that light would be bent by gravity. Indeed it was, as the famous experiment in 1921 or 1922, was it 1919? showed — that light from Mercury in an eclipse was bent by the sun. Now, when we begin to consider these wholly concentrated implosions of matter which have more mass than the sun, they must pull everything into them. Everything disappears. You cannot ever see these particular stars, which are called black holes in space, because everything goes into it, and comes out where, somewhere else. Hm?

That is a more curious model of the universe than we're used to considering. Now physics deals with notions of matter and antimatter. Is it so outrageous then to speak of death as having a life which has as many laws as life?

STRATTON: Existential states of death.

MAILER: Existential states of death. Exactly. We speak of the speed of light as being 186,000 miles a second and nothing can go faster than that. Except yesterday we were talking about, what if God is there to give a grace so speed can go faster? What if anti-matter lives on the other side of the speed of light? We live in a universe of such peculiar immensity and intimacy.

As we see more and more into these notions, the differences between the mightiest phenomena and the tiniest seem to have almost nothing to do with space. It's as if finally space becomes no more than our metaphorical incapacity to comprehend. Throw that out. It's rather as if space becomes no more than the measure of our inability to comprehend that every process, large and small, is without meaning as a process which is large or small in itself, because everything exists in its reverberation upon everything else. One atom, one most special atom, may have more significance than a star. So we inhabit a universe which is fell with purpose. And therefore must try to create, or at least try to exercise, our profoundest notion of champions and villains, of enemies and new gods within it. Theology will yet prove more amazing than science.

That's where I would like to let this rest. That any view we take of technology has to deal with the principle, that it is either a manifest of God or the Devil or else is some dissertation of purpose or malignity from that universe outside them which gives every suggestion of being a juggler's paradise. Because it can turn its pockets inside out.

1974

Existential Aesthetics

An Interview with Laura Adams

❧

LAURA ADAMS: Since the late 1950s you've had a vision of God and the Devil at war for possession of the universe, a vision that has been the metaphysical and moral center of your work. Has that vision changed appreciably over the years?

NORMAN MAILER: I don't know the answer. When you deal with cosmology, the question becomes on the one hand enormous — do God and the Devil war in the galaxies? — yet is intimate on the other. Since we all have our own idea of God and the Devil, it's hard for the idea not to change, even fluctuate. I'd say that over the last ten or fifteen years I've kept going back and forth in my mind over a notion that's hard to formulate, and I don't know that I should try — it's the sort of thing that sounds silly unless you can write a book about it — but for the purpose of this answer, just let me say that if there is a war continuing between God and the Devil for humankind, for the *future* of humankind, then this war is much more complex than a simple confrontation. We have to ask ourselves what the role of technology is in all this, and I've had years when I've believed technology is an instrument of the Devil, other years in which I've seen God in a Faustian contract with technology. Technology is perhaps some third force, some element that's come into our universe from other universes. Now all this is too endlessly and chronically paranoid to try to get into it in the form of an interview. I think you can dramatize these notions in a major novel, but only a major novel. You would wreck a minor novel by introducing such ideas. Therefore to talk about it in an interview is hopeless. It leads to people saying you have a windmill for a brain. Still I can see by the look in your eye that you're hardly ready to give up.

ADAMS: Isn't it an obsession, a form of paranoia, or even atavistic to think that there are cosmic forces manipulating us for their own ends?

MAILER: Well, I've never felt we are the simple creatures of these forces. On the contrary, I think they are fighting for our allegiance or even our unwitting cooperation. It isn't only that man needs God, but recall us to the title of that old French movie, *God Needs Men*. (Of course you couldn't use such a title today. You'd have to say "God Needs *Persons*.") Here's what I'm trying to say: To the degree I have any intense religious notion it's that when we fail God we are not merely disappointing some mightily benign paterfamilias who'd hoped we might turn out well and didn't. We are literally bleeding God, we're leeching Him, depriving Him of *His* vision. You see, I start with the idea that the explanation for our situation on earth may be that we are part of a divine vision which is not, necessarily, all loving, but on the contrary is a vision which wishes to take us out across the stars — a vision of existence at war with other varieties of existence in the cosmos. By this light, flying saucers may be, or may represent, a certain unconscious human awareness that there is this possibility in the universe, that there are other forms of intelligence which have nothing to do with us. Nothing even to do with our divinities.

ADAMS: Do you know the Arthur C. Clarke novel, *Childhood's End*?

MAILER: No.

ADAMS: In it the human race mutates into an essence, a form of energy, that unites with a kind of benevolent Oversoul which, interestingly, has used another race of benevolent beings in the form of devils to prepare the way for the human mutants. It appears that our fear of devils was based on a premonition that they would have something to do with the dissolution of our race. The unconscious awareness you spoke of reminded me of this. But isn't this notion that, as D.J. expressed it in *Why Are We in Vietnam?*, "You never know what vision has been humping you through the night," contradictory to the perception of good and evil in *An American Dream*? There it seemed that good and evil were for the most part clearly demarcated, known to Rojack. Deborah and Barney Kelly were evil; Cherry was good.

MAILER: That was his view of it.

ADAMS: His view of it?

MAILER: That was all it was — Rojack's view of it. To the degree a reader sympathizes with Rojack, that would be the reader's view of it. To the degree a reader decides that Rojack is an absurd hero, he won't go along with that view. But even assuming that Rojack's view had something to do with *my* view of the characters, I was certainly attempting to make Deborah more complex on any spectrum of good and evil than Barney Kelly. Barney Kelly was supposed to be the focus of evil in the book.

ADAMS: The Devil personified.

MAILER: Well, the Devil approached, anyway. Whereas Deborah was someone who was, in quotes, "in thrall" to the Devil. But a woman of complexity, not altogether unacquainted with goodness.

ADAMS: And Cherry?

MAILER: I didn't mean Cherry to be all good by any means. To the degree that she's better than she ought to be, she's too sentimental a character. A gangster's moll is not the simplest kind of goodness we arrive at. But I wanted to indicate some characters had more purchase on good than others.

ADAMS: Cherry seemed to have a hard kernel of goodness even though she was surrounded by corruption.

MAILER: I think she's finally an enigmatic character. In my opinion, she's the weakest character in *An American Dream*. I think people who don't like the book have their strongest argument starting with Cherry. To a great degree, I'm afraid she's a sentimental conception. We don't really know much about her. We're asked to believe that this goodness exists in her but we don't have any idea of the real play of good and evil in her. She's a shadowy figure. Of course, my cop-out is that she's seen through Rojack's eyes. He's in an incandescent state of huge paranoia and enormous awareness. He's more heroic and more filled with dread than at any point in his life. So she seems like a lighthouse in the fog. What else does one do in such a state but fall madly in love for twenty-four hours and lose the love? It would have taken more wit than I possessed to have made her a character of dimension under these circumstances. Perhaps she did have to appear as a sentimental figure. Still I think there's no getting around it, she's the first weakness of the book.

ADAMS: But it's a highly metaphorical novel. One of the mistakes many critics made in first reviewing it was to take it too literally. Isn't Cherry seen metaphorically as love, the reward of courage?

MAILER: Well, no. I don't believe a metaphorical novel has any right to exist until it exists on its ground floor. You know I never start with my characters as symbols. I'm unhappy if I can't see my characters. I mean, I not only have to know what they look like, and how tall they are, whether they're good looking or plain, but I also like to have some idea of what they smell like. So I had a pretty good idea of Cherry *physically*, a very clear idea in fact, but I would have been happier if her character had emerged somewhat more. I think Deborah, for instance, is vastly more successful. Deborah is worthy of a book in herself. In fact, at one time I thought idly of doing a book on Deborah, and then chose not to. But how she drew coincidences to herself. One of the things about *An American Dream* that's not often realized is my little theory, if you will, that as events become more dramatic so does the play of coincidence become more intense. You can reverse it. You can say that coincidence may fail to occur unless events are dramatic. I think there's a reason for that. If you believe in Gods and Devils, and I choose the plural because not only is God on one side, Devil on the other but they certainly have armies, adjutants, aides, little demons, angels, well, when important events occur why wouldn't they be concerned? Why wouldn't they be present? Why not try to tip the scales? Why wouldn't God and the Devil have their department of dirty tricks? You know, see them as some sort of sublime extension of the CIA.

ADAMS: That is why I see the novel as so highly metaphorical. The kinds of experiences Rojack has, the vision of shooting arrows into Cherry's womb while she's singing in the night club, for example, seem to me to exist in a dream allegory but not at the literal level.

MAILER: I would disagree. I'd had the experience of being in night clubs and thinking evil thoughts and really barbing them like darts and sending them to people and seeing them react. At the time I didn't know whether I was profoundly drunk or, you know, was I all alone in the world? But I had to recognize that there was a psychic reality to it. It wasn't just a fantasy. Since then, there's been any amount, my god, there's so much material now to indicate that this is not at all unreasonable. For one thing, we do have telepathic powers, we talk about the human aura, about the ability to send hostile vibrations, everybody uses that phrase, but, you know, if you can send a hostile vibration, which is to say, a hostile wave, why not employ modern theories of light and say hate appears not only in the form of a wave but also as a particle? If you can do it with light, you can do it with hate. In other words, send a damn particle into someone. Why not assume you can sting someone with a thought so concentrated that they'll turn around and rub the back of their neck? I invite people who are reading this interview to try it from time to time. It helps if you're drunk, of course.

ADAMS: Is that what you've been doing to tape recorders all these years?

MAILER: Oh, I think there's a good reason why tape recorders bomb out on me. Why not assume we have electrical powers — we know there are pictures taken of the human aura in Russia. What is it called, the Kirlian process? Did you ever notice when you're in a real hurry to make a phone call, and you've got one of those button phones where you can dial quickly, that if you dial too quickly with too much desire, you never get your number?

ADAMS: Yes.

MAILER: Then you have to stop and say, "Okay, I don't really care if I get the number or not," and dial more slowly. Then the phone becomes your servant again. It's as if there's an electrical resistance to your electrical intensity.

ADAMS: I simply assumed the computer couldn't handle the digits as fast as I could push them.

MAILER: Well, I notice it with a dial phone, too. The phenomenon is not only in the speed with which you dial, but the intensity with which you want to get that call through. It's almost as if there is something in the center of electricity that mocks us. I've felt this with all sorts of electrical phenomena. It's possible I'm more charged, have more electricity about me. I don't mean that as any agreeable or attractive condition, it's bound to be disagreeable, but possibly I could have more effect upon electrical instruments than other people, a little more effect, ten percent more, whatever. At any rate, to go back to *An American Dream*, my point is that there wasn't a single phenomenon in that book that I considered dreamlike or fanciful or fantastical. To me, it was a realistic book, but a realistic book at that place where extraordinary things are happening. I believe the experience of extraordinary people in extraordinary situations is not like our ordinary realistic experience at all. For example, one of the reasons I've never written about great prizefighters in a novel is that the experience they have in the ring is, I think, considerably different from what we believe it is. More intense, more mystical, more "spooky" if you will, than anything we see on the outside. Who wants to write about a fight the way sportswriters do, or even as fighters discuss it after the fight: "I was waiting to set him up with a good right. He dropped his guard and I popped him." That's the way they talk. Only, it isn't their experience.

ADAMS: I grant you that the characters in *An American Dream* perceive and experience reality altogether differently from us ordinary folks. Still, it seems to me that their literal reality has a metaphorical level as well, just as your literal realities nearly always turn into metaphorical ones linked to the central set of metaphors regarding the existence of God or the Devil. I've come to see them as metaphors for our moral directions, which in the absence of absolutes become existential, unknowable as good or evil.

MAILER: My metaphors explain more phenomena to me than any theology I can adopt. I was an atheist for years because I couldn't stomach the notion of the all-good, all-powerful God who calmly watched all sorts of suffering which by any extension of our human imagination could not be productive of anything, not even productive of future karma. In other words that whole waste of human possibilities of the most grinding, grim, dull sort. It seems to me that the only explanation is God is not all-powerful: He's merely doing the best He can.

ADAMS: But how literally does God exist?

MAILER: I believe He exists literally.

ADAMS: How?

MAILER: It's not for me to know how or where He exists. It's reasonable to assume He exists in a great many ways, in places we can comprehend and a great many where we cannot. All I'm saying is that He does not have to be all-powerful. What is there that makes Him all-powerful? He was powerful enough to have created our solar system, perhaps. And if you ask what are His limits, that might be my guess. But this is babbling. It isn't important where God's limits are. What's significant is the idea that God is not all-powerful, nor is the Devil. Rather it is that we exist as some mediating level between them. You see, this notion does restore a certain dignity to moral choice.

ADAMS: Of course, it does.

MAILER: It becomes important whether you're good or bad.

ADAMS: In trying to know what is good or evil aren't you in effect trying to take existentialism to its logical end, that is, to end existentialism?

MAILER: Not end it, seat it. Of all the philosophies, existentialism approaches experience with the greatest awe: it says we can't categorize experience before we've experienced it. The only way we're going to be able to discover what the truth about anything might be is to submit ourselves to the reality of the experience. At the same time, given its roots in atheistic philosophers like Sartre, existentialism has always tended toward the absurd. By way of Sartre, we are to act as if there were a purpose to things even though we know there is not. And that has become the general concept of existentialism in America. But it's not mine. I'm an existentialist who believes there is a God and a Devil at war with one another. Like Sartre in his atheism, I offer a statement of absolute certainty equally founded on the inability to verify it. Atheism is as removed from logical positivism as theology. Still, I don't give a goddamn if I can verify this or not. There has to be something out there beyond logical positivism. I want my brain to live. I want to adventure out on a few thoughts. The fact that I can never demonstrate them is not nearly so important to me as the fact that I may come up with an hypothesis so simple, so central, that I may be able to apply it in thousands of situations. If it begins to give me some inner coherence, if I begin to think that I know more as a result of this philosophy, why not?

ADAMS: But isn't what you've identified as existentialism, extended to its logical end, seeking to know what is finally unknowable?

MAILER: That's not my definition of existentialism. I'd say we find ourselves in an existential situation whenever we are in a situation where we cannot foretell the end. Some of these situations are grave. If you get into a skid on an icy road, at a speed that's uncomfortably high, you don't know if you're going to be able to pull your car out of it without a smack-up. That's an existential situation. When people talk about it afterward they think of that quality of time when it is slowing up. The first time people connect with marijuana — not the first or the twentieth time they smoke it, but the first time they *connect* with it — they're in an existential situation. It's not the universe they have been sitting on all the time. It's slower, more sensuous, more meaningful, more natural, but filled with awe. The light tends to have a little of the hour of the wolf, a light close to a lavender or purple, that light you get on certain kinds of evenings, or very early on certain kinds of dawns full of foreboding. But it's — there are all kinds of situations. A woman losing her virginity is in an existential situation. Of course, part of the comedy of twentieth-century technology is that it's gotten to the point where a woman can lose her virginity without being in an existential situation for a moment. It's all exactly the way she thought it was going to be, she's been so well oriented.

ADAMS: I think that assumes that her partner is not also a virgin. . . . All right. Your basic existential situation is a situation anyone enters at any moment in time when the end result of his actions is unknown. But isn't to a larger extent your aim in all the work that you've been doing to uncover what is essentially good or evil in our natures and God's nature when that kind of thing is actually unknowable? What I was going to suggest earlier in talking about the demarcations of good and evil in *An American Dream* is that you seem to have become increasingly obsessed since that time with your inability to know what is good and what is evil.

MAILER: You say I'm obsessed, but where would be the literary proof of that? What books would show that?

ADAMS: Start with the case of Richard Nixon in *Miami and the Siege of Chicago* and *St. George and the Godfather*: your inability to know or to intuit whether Nixon is basically good or basically evil; to know, in *Of a Fire on the Moon*, whether our space program will carry God's vision to the stars or the Devil's; to know in *Why Are We in Vietnam?* whether America has made a Faustian compact with the Devil or whether God is using us for evil ends; whether or not our national leaders and events win or lose us ground in this divine battle. It seems to me that you lead us to this question, with increasing desire to know the answer, in every work.

MAILER: Well, it could be said that all I'm doing is leading people back to Kierkegaard. I'd remind you I've written this several times: Kierkegaard taught us, or tried to teach us, that at that moment we're feeling most saintly, we may in fact be evil. And that moment when we think we're most evil and finally corrupt, we may, in fact, in the eyes of God, be saintly at that moment. The first value of this notion is that it strips us of that fundamental arrogance of assuming that at any given moment any of us have enough centrality, have a *seat* from which we can expound our dogma, or measure our moral value. So we don't have the right to say Richard Nixon is: A. good; B. evil. I might have my opinion of Richard Nixon, but I don't have the right to say that man is evil, any more than I have a right to say he is good.

ADAMS: Do you have a clear notion of the good?

MAILER: No. But I have, if you will, I have and I submit to the force of this word, I have a fairly well-formed *cloud* of intuitions about the nature of the good, and, like a cloud, it has to a certain degree a structure, and yet the structure is capable of altering quickly, depending on the celestial winds blowing and the less celestial winds. A cloud changes shape quickly but it remains a cloud. It's not just simply an unformed chaos.

ADAMS: You've said that an evil person is someone who has a clear notion of the good and operates in opposition to it.

MAILER: Therefore by my own definition I'm definitely not evil.

ADAMS: All right, but are you wicked?

MAILER: Unquestionably wicked, yes.

ADAMS: By your own terms, which is not knowing what is good or evil in any situation, but upping the ante each time.

MAILER: Upping the ante, yes. I'd say I may be one of the most wicked spirits in American life today. Maybe. America may be changing faster than I am.

ADAMS: Is it fair to say that your existentialism is leading us to know the nature of good and evil?

ADAMS: It's leading us to — well, let me take a detour. People who submit to logical positivism, and go on from there into philosophies as difficult as Wittgenstein's, will answer if you ask, "Why go through these incredible disciplines in order to verify the fact that you're able to verify the wing span of a gnat but not of an archangel?" They will answer, "Well, it isn't what we are able to verify that is interesting, so much as that we go through a discipline which enables us to think cogently. We're less likely to go in for sloppy thinking thereafter." That's the value of it. I'd say by going in for my variety of associational, metaphorical thinking (which is, of course, the exact opposite) I may be able eventually to think speculatively without feeling philosophical vertigo. You see, it doesn't take any more illogic to posit that there's a god or devil than it takes to say there is none. The latter statement is absolutely as potent an act of faith. There's a marvelous line in *Jumpers*, the play by Tom Stoppard, to that effect. I paraphrase:

"Well, maybe atheism is that crutch people need to protect themselves against having to face the enormity of the existence of God." You know, once you contemplate the notion that there is God and this God may be embattled, the terror you feel is enormous.

ADAMS: It's a terror, but isn't it also paranoia?

MAILER: No. The terror is not that some force is working on you to ruin you. It's another kind of terror: It's that nothing is nailed down. That we are out there — that our lives are truly existential. That we're not going to end up well. Not necessarily. You see, there's always been this sort of passive confidence implicit in Christianity, the confidence that things are going to work out all right. One does have to die, that's true, but if one keeps one's nose reasonably clean, one is going to heaven. That gave security to everybody. The ship of state was built on that security. The ship of state was nailed down. It didn't travel the stormy seas. Rather, it was carried by the strongest pallbearers of the nation. And what's happened now is we're entering an existential period in our history where nothing is nailed down. All the American faiths, one by one, are being exploded. We lived for too long in a paranoid dream world that believed communism was the secret of all evil on earth because it was the social embodiment of the Devil.

ADAMS: That's paranoid.

MAILER: That's paranoid. But I don't believe the Devil is the secret of all evil on earth. I believe something more complicated than that. I think God might be the source of a considerable amount of evil. Because if God is embattled, He could fail to take care, much to His great woe, of people who are devoted to Him, in the same way that a general might have to surrender soldiers on a hill. And those soldiers could give up with great bitterness in their hearts.

ADAMS: You've talked about evil in one sense as God's shit, God's excrement.

MAILER: Where did I say that?

ADAMS: It comes up in "The Metaphysics of the Belly." A colleague of mine once remarked that it's but a step from scatology to eschatology and I've often thought of this remark with regard to your work. Now I'm interested in the relationship between excrement and eternity. If God's shit is evil, but shit is associated with the Devil, doesn't this imply that God creates evil?

MAILER: There are references in my work to the idea that shit and the Devil have an umbilical relation, but it's not my idea after all. Luther had a few notions about it.

ADAMS: As did Jonathan Swift.

MAILER: It's an idea that goes — it starts with the most primitive peoples. It goes all the way. There's a reason for it. Shit is what we reject, at least to the degree that the shit felt it deserved a better end for itself. In other words, a lot of our shit has nutrients in it, worth in it. It's just that the body couldn't take it, and so passed it out. Some of the best of the food goes out with the shit as well as some of the worst. That's what I said in "The Metaphysics of the Belly." All right. To the degree that we can loosen our imagination to assume this stuff might have a soul, after all we're beginning to discover now that plants have feelings and souls, so it may be that food, even though in a peculiar relation to life, not as alive as a plant, let's say, or as an animal, but still alive to a degree, has a mood, has a spirit, has something. If food feels it has been violated, suppose it can die with a curse. Of course, the Devil loves to be around and pick up those who die with a curse. Malcolm Muggeridge once had Mother Theresa of Calcutta on a television show with him. Muggeridge, who is by any measure a devoutly religious man, had just written a book about Mother Theresa and obviously revered her. He told me what she used to do in Calcutta. Her order of nuns would take people who were dying on the street and move them into her convent where they'd die anyway a few days later — they didn't begin to have medicine to take care of them or anything like that — but her notion was, and Muggeridge was moved by this, and I agree that it is a moving idea, was that she didn't want them to die with absolutely nothing. She wanted them to be able to come in and get a little attention before they died so they wouldn't go out with a complete bitterness in their hearts. Now that is a religious woman. The recognition that one not die with a curse is fundamental to any inquiry into what could be the possible nature of God and the Devil. If God is embattled, and can't give fair justice to all, then what of those who do not achieve what they saw as their own fulfillment and thereby become spiritual material for the Devil, if not in this life then in another? We haven't said one word about karma, but my first idea these days is that any attempt to speak of these things makes no sense unless you take into account the peculiar calculus of karma. We may have to recognize that we're not only acting for this life but for other lives. Our past lives and our future lives. Paying dues, receiving awards. Reducing the cost of future dues, for example, by certain acts of abnegation that make no sense to us or our friends, yet ready to dare, on the other hand, sometimes desperate activities because we *are* desperate. The condition in which we live is hurting our karma.

ADAMS: Karma is a word you've used increasingly in the last few years. It's a term that you did not use in "The Metaphysics of the Belly" or "The Political Economy of Time," but which you could have in describing the nature of the soul. Is this something new in your metaphysics or is it a term for something that you've already described, like the way in which the soul exists, in "The Political Economy of Time"?

MAILER: I had come across the word in books but never paid any attention. In about 1953, I think it was in Robinson, Illinois, I went out to visit James Jones in his writers' colony and he and Lowney Handy were talking about karma and I said, "What's all that?" So he gave me the standard explanation which is that we are not only reincarnated, but the way in which we are is the reflection, the judgment, the truth, of how we lived our previous life. If you exist in a simple form of karma with no interference by Gods or Devils, a natural flux of karma, then to the degree you lived a life that was artful, your reincarnation was artful. To the degree you lived a life that destroyed the time of others and dredged up all the swamp muds, so you are a creature of the swamp in your next life. The beauty of this may be that there is now good purpose to the swamp. (This isn't Jones's talk any longer, just a more general explanation of karma.) At any rate, Jones went on about it and I said, "You *believe* in that?" Because I was an atheist and a socialist in those days. He said, "Oh, sure. That's the only thing that makes sense." Well, the line rang in my head for years. "The only thing that makes sense." I thought about it over and over and in the last three or four years I began to think, "Yes, that does make sense. Jones was right."

1975

Marriage

An Interview with Buzz Farbar

BUZZ FARBAR: In your book on Marilyn Monroe, you say of her marriage to Arthur Miller, "It was only a few marriages (which is to say a few failures) later that he [Mailer] could recognize how he would have done no better than Miller, and probably have been damaged further in the process." Why do you feel a few marriages can be equated with a few failures?

NORMAN MAILER: People used to go into marriage without questioning the institution, never thought of a life where they might not be married. By now, weddings are beleaguered. When people go into it today, we have an existential adventure, for they don't know how it will turn out. In other words, marriage has become interesting again. It's a gamble they well may lose. Of course, I'm not referring to all of society — more to that educated leisure class which is the base of the establishment. Precisely in that part of our world, marriage is weakest.

So, in a sense, such men and women are gambling against a social tide. They're saying: We're going to make this marriage work, even though ten thousand obstacles in the scheme of things fight against us. Including almost everybody's greater desire for promiscuity. So it may be legitimate to speak of a marriage that's terminated, as a failure. Like a lost bet.

FARBAR: How about the termination of a bad marriage? Is being able to end it a failure or a success?

MAILER: Obviously there are all kinds of marriages. I suppose I was referring to people who are relatively independent, and sufficiently narcissistic to want to live their own kind of life. For them to be able to live with someone else is not an automatic venture. But then you can always find men and women who get married out of deep dependence on one another. Such marriages are usually a tyranny on one side, an enslavement on the other. Sometimes they are awful marriages where it may be a victory for the weak mate to split.

FARBAR: Do you feel you learned something from each marriage? Does each marriage get better, or worse, or is it all the same?

MAILER: Oh, each marriage is different. Being married to a woman is the equivalent, I think, of living in a major culture. Should you find yourself married to one woman and then to another, you have gone through the equivalent of spending five years in England after five years in France.

I don't look back on these marriages with bitterness. It seems to me you often get as much as you lost. I even discovered there may be four stages to knowing a woman. First, there's living together. It's often thought equal to marriage. Not by half. You can live with a woman and never begin to comprehend her at all, not until you get married to her. Once you do that, you're in the next stage. The third, obviously, is children. Once again your woman is different. Say it's analogous to a culture going through major transformations. The fourth stage is knowing a woman once you're divorced. Then, indeed, you come to know something at last. So if it weren't for the fact that there are children, there would be something almost agreeable about moving from marriage to marriage, just as there is something exciting about spending five years in England and five in France.

But there are children, and that's the vortex of all postmarital pain, which is always so surprisingly huge. Because finally the children come out of a vision in the marriage. It doesn't always even matter how casually they may have been conceived. Children can be created out of desperation, out of laziness, out of apathy, as a sporting proposition. But, usually, children come out of some covert union, some feeling that you have something together which should be embodied in a child. Otherwise, it's a little absurd to conceive. Therefore, once you have children, if the marriage breaks you can speak of it as failure. The vision that's embodied in that child is now broken. Not to count the damage to the child.

FARBAR: Knowing you as well as I do, I know that you are, to use your word "profoundly," a profoundly moral person —

MAILER: Can I interrupt you? I'm usually called a profoundly moral person by people who are trying to startle others who say I'm immoral or amoral, people who don't know much about my work and think of me as some sort of sexual ogre. Of course, my defenders then say, "On the contrary, he's a very moral man." I don't consider myself moral at all. I see myself as a man who lives in an embattled relation to morality. In other words, it isn't so much that I am moral, as that I have an advanced sensibility toward what may be moral and immoral in my actions. Which I find intolerable as a result, because I know when I'm being immoral, and I'm being immoral most of the time. By my own lights. In other words, I'm so rarely true to my own code that it's hard to maintain any self-respect. But I would never speak of myself as a moral man. Quite the contrary.

FARBAR: Can you love deeply more than one woman? If you're committed to one woman, how do you feel about a relationship with another one at the same time? Do you feel good or bad during an affair?

MAILER: I think it's impossible to be in love with two women at the same time. By now, in the middle of the twentieth century, so few of us get anywhere near that kind of love that it seems a sentimental fallacy. Just think of the people we know. Think of speaking to them of love. A titter runs through the table. What does it mean to most people when you talk about being in love with two people at once? It means you're fucking two women at once, that's all it means.

But if you're really in love with a woman, I think it's almost impossible to be in love with another. If you love a woman, you are engaged in a vision with her. That rarely happens. Maybe two, three, four times in our lives. But once you do, every time you give something to another woman, the beginning of a different vision is being sent to a different place. It can only work successfully when you have people whose souls are neatly separated. I believe we all have divided souls, but few of us have souls that are divided formally — in other words, Dr. Jekyll and Mr. Hyde. Those two psyches can have two great love affairs, yes. But most of us have double personalities that are more amorphous. The edges interreact. They're never clear-cut. And it's not simple for us to decide what our two personalities might be. The borders are not clear to us. As a result, being in love with two people usually muddies the distinction further.

FARBAR: Getting back to the Monroe book. You say, "It's no accident that studs are usually heartless about the aftermath. By their logic they've already treated the mother well and given the baby a good beginning."

MAILER: That's the stud's vanity. He's given a woman what she needs. We start with the natural assumption that studs are male chauvinists. Obviously, I was trying to explore one facet of that. Other people think, "God, he's a heartless man, he went in and knocked that woman up, walked away, never thought twice about it, he never bothered. How can anyone be that inhuman, that brutal?" I was trying to look for the stud's own self-justification. Wouldn't it come out as, "After all the pleasure I gave that woman, she has no cause for complaint"? To me, there's something a hint comic to it. Anybody who knows anything about women can recognize that the pleasure we assume we are giving to them can be a little less, in most cases, than we assumed.

FARBAR: There's always that little bit of doubt in a stud's mind, too.

MAILER: Oh, of course. You know studs, they're like professional athletes. They don't think of all the guys who can't make love. They think of other studs. They live in the terror that some other dude might be a little better than them. They're like street fighters.

FARBAR: You write about Monroe that "she can be tender, yet cold-blooded — her love tends to end when the role ends." Generally a woman is more cold-blooded than a man. Why is this so?

MAILER: A man is in a more existential position than a woman, he has to get an erection. The act doesn't take place in crackerjack fashion without that erection. So there is a limit to how much a man can simulate in sex. Unless a woman is suffering from a vagina so dry it's impossible for a man to enter her, she can simulate, and throw out a huge number of passions without feeling one. Much harder for a man to pretend to great sexual excitement if he's not feeling it. So it may not be that women are more cold-blooded than men so much as it's easier for women to get away with it.

FARBAR: You say of the marriage of Miller and Monroe, "Actually, they settle into good days and bad days. Which is the narrative line of marriage."

MAILER: Well, you could speak of certain human relations as being comparable to literary forms. For instance, the one-night stand was like a poem, good or bad. An affair of reasonable duration, a short story. By this logic, a marriage is a novel. In a short story we're interested in the point. In a novel we usually follow the way people move from drama to boredom back to drama again. And we often judge a novelist by his skill in moving people in and out of these high and low areas of existence. Of course, marriage is exactly like that. In a marriage, our interest is not that a given point is made in a given night, but the way that recognition is confirmed or eroded over the weeks or months to follow. The narrative line of all marriage, in that sense, is good days and bad days. And most people like to live in the form of a novel. Just as there are people who like to live in the form of the short story.

FARBAR: And psychopaths?

MAILER: They have lives that consist of poems, mostly bummers. But a majority of people seem to prefer endless, meaningless days. They don't want the ups to be so high they can't manage to come down to a life of lower pressure. They are the people who love marriage precisely because it offers an agreeable way to live in a slightly bored state. They seek out boredom, because it relieves them of dread. A mild boredom, not an intense boredom. An intense boredom, of course, is a form of torture.

FARBAR: Do you think that a man, when he is making love to a woman, is always measuring himself in some way, or is he being measured by the woman?

MAILER: Competitive men are obviously going to measure themselves against other men. Many women will have, perhaps, their own private scores for the man. But when a woman is in love, a man can be . . . well, in the sense of a sexual athlete, he can be unpromising, yet he can seem sublime to a woman, because she is open to him. The most tentative caress he offers arouses feeling that more skillful men won't. Obviously, sexual pleasure is not simply related to performance. Otherwise, we would have sexual Olympics. If people are not in love, but happen to like sex as a sport, the way other people like horses or skiing or motorboat racing, then performance comes to the fore. It was my assumption that when Marilyn fell in love, her man became sublime. For a time at least. In fact, it's usually necessary, in love, to believe that the man or woman you're with is better than anyone who has come before, so we find that way in which they are better than others. We have a need to believe our sex life is becoming more alive all the time. Otherwise, it's hard to continue. Especially as you get older.

FARBAR: Do you feel, as I do, that when a woman says to you, "So-and-so is a lousy lay," you then feel ill-will toward her? Is that purely a male ego thing, not wanting to hear that another man was a bad lay?

MAILER: I'd say we usually take pleasure in hearing another man is a bad lay. But if we have any sense, we recognize it's mostly meaningless. If you hear all over town that a certain man is a bad lay from just about every woman who has spoken about him, there's a reasonable assumption the guy is not too good. But would you like to be described by a woman on the worst night you ever had in bed? Or any of the hundred worst nights? I dread to think of certain descriptions of me. Speaking just of perform-ance, we have a spectrum. So when a woman says of a given man that he was a bad lay, I wince. Unless there's real cause, the woman is usually avenging herself. But then we know that women, maybe out of self-protection, lie a vast amount in sex, even lie to themselves about the past. We have all seen women who couldn't keep their hands off their man; then the years went by, and the man was out of her life. Slowly his sexual reputation sank, inch by inch. A part of the comedy of sexual affairs.

FARBAR: I wonder what your feelings are about promiscuity in women. And promiscuity in men.

MAILER: I suppose I believe you pay for every last thing you get out of life. Years ago, Calder Willingham told me a story about a situ-ation where he tried every trick to make a woman leave him. Fi-nally she began going with another man. Then he discovered he was jealous. He told this story on himself with great humor, and looked at me and said, "Norman, you can't cheat life." He said this in his inimitable Georgia accent. It's not a remark one hasn't heard before. But there's such a thing as hearing a maxim at just the right moment for oneself. Then it goes all the way in. So that remark stayed with me. Whenever I'm trying to work out some sort of moral balance for myself, I find the thought useful.

Of course, certain people get more out of being promiscuous than others, and pay less for it. But the idea that people can be promiscuous without exploiting their own sensitivity is impossi-ble. On the other hand, promiscuity is altogether necessary for some, especially if you have a personality that consists of frag-ments, as most of us do by now. We live in a time of interruption. The art of the absurd is built on the fact that we live in a continuum of interruption. Turn on the television and see a story slam into an advertisement, and so forth. As a result, there's a huge tendency to become fragmented. Then different relations give us different things in different places.

But as you get older, you begin to discover that promiscuity gets more and more difficult, because it makes you commit too much of yourself. I'm fifty now. I've reached the point where conceivably I could be making love to a woman and die in bed. That can happen. If it did, which woman would I be with? Does one want to die with a stranger? As you get older, making love becomes more apocalyptic exactly because you're closer to the end of your life each time. As a result there's less desire to be promiscuous. On the other hand, if people are rooted in the promiscuous, the attempt to keep themselves monogamous can induce all sorts of neuroses and diseases, no question.

What I distrust always, however, are professional swingers. Come on, join the gangfuck, it's good for you. Those people are as totalitarian as the ones who say chastity is the only good on earth. By now, they're more. Part of the totalitarian is to make an absolute out of the prevailing tendency of the time.

FARBAR: But if you pick up a girl in a bar at three in the morning and have a flying fuck at four and go home at five or six, that to me is not promiscuity. It's just something that happened. It's almost a physical act, like going to the bathroom. Don't you feel that?

MAILER: Yeah, but I hate it. Look, there are times when one has to depart from one's identity. As in *Last Tango in Paris* people making love without identity is exciting. Obviously, there is a need to treat sex as a species of evacuation. We've all had great fucks with people we hardly know. While that satisfies something, by now I hate it. Hate having too much sexual pleasure without feeling a great deal for the woman. I tend by now to stay away from fucking a girl I don't love but really enjoy fucking. I used to like that years ago, loved the power, but by now I kind of hate it. I hate the feeling afterward. I don't hate the fuck. I love the fuck, but I hate what comes afterward.

FARBAR: Because of the way you think she must feel when she knows it's a dead end?

MAILER: No. I'm not even thinking about her. Well, I'm thinking about her in the sense that I'm a guilty enough man so that I can't use people around me much anymore. We were speaking about morality earlier, and it isn't that I'm moral, it's almost rather that

I have enough respect for morality to feel I can't abuse the edges of it forever, can't abuse some of my central premises forever. I have this belief in karmic balance — that we come into life with a soul that carries an impost of guilt and reward from the past. And at the end of each life we may be reborn, which I think is a reward in itself. Which not everyone gets. Some people's souls die, literally die, just as the body dies; some people's souls die in a given life. As you know, I believe in two kinds of death. Final death as some species of oblivion, and transcendental death, where you're reborn in some other form of existence that gives fair measure for your previous lives. So I think as we get older there comes a time when we have to worry about this moral balance in ourselves. Maybe I've come to the point where I can't use people anymore. I do know it leaves me depressed to think I've had a woman for too little, offered no real feeling. I tend to stay away from such women. That wasn't true years ago.

FARBAR: That leads me to another question. How have you been able to maintain such extraordinarily good relationships with three of your four ex-wives? They truly seem to be your good friends. It's more than just being civilized, it's a special kind of talent, I think.

MAILER: I think we loved each other. I certainly loved each of them, and I believe they loved me. We have children together, and we love those children. When we broke up there was a recognition . . . well, we broke up for different reasons each time, but there was a recognition that there had to be something low about making the children suffer.

Of course, each time the marriage broke up, it was hardly agreeable or nice. Maybe over the years we've come together a little. When you're divorced from a woman, the friendship can then start. Because one's sexual vanity is not in it any longer. At least not in the same way. You can look back on it and say, "Yes, we were pretty good together, but not good enough." And let it go at that. Then, of course, everything in the woman you liked in the first place, her charm, the more attractive aspects of her character, now can come back into play, as well as everything that got lost in the harassments of marriage. A hint of tenderness returns.

When you're in love, the stakes are high. There's much more anger when there's love. Because if one's love is frustrated, it means a good deal more than if one's liking is balked. So there's a readiness in marriage to walk around in a state of resentment which starts to flatten all the smaller affections. Of course, there are marriages where the opposite occurs. When the sexual impulse quiets down or dies even, the people become great friends. Carnally speaking, they're divorced, but they don't separate legally. They live together as dear friends. Such marriages are often nice. I've never been in one, but I imagine it could be very nice.

FARBAR: Let's change the subject completely. I wondered how you felt about lesbianism. If you had any thought that you could —

MAILER: It's funny, you know, I've always had a puritanical attitude about homosexuality, almost as if I couldn't afford to begin to get homosexual, because God knows where it would all stop. You know about that old Talmudic notion, that if you want to restrain an impulse don't just build a fence around the impulse itself, build a fence around the fence. By analogy, I've never been tolerant of the idea of homosexuality for myself. But I've always had the feeling that if I were a woman, that I somehow would enjoy lesbianism. I think if I were a woman it would mean very little to me to be a lesbian part of the time.

FARBAR: Is that because lesbian women you've known or read about are always saying they know how to do whatever it is they're doing better than men do?

MAILER: Well, obviously there must be fine sensuality among lesbians. Listen, what am I edging around it for? I have seen women together and it's lovely. Or, let us say, it is lovely provided it isn't finally designed to exclude men from every relation with women.

FARBAR: Last spring, in a piece in *New York Review of Books* on *Last Tango* you wrote about Brando and Maria Schneider being nameless when they meet each other, and this made their sexual relationship intriguing. As soon as some sort of relationship begins, and they get to know one another's names, it ends. Why do women enjoy anonymous sex?

MAILER: I think once a woman becomes anonymous in a sexual relationship — it's as if she's weightless. She no longer has the gravity of old responsibility. She can cut loose.

But I think one thing's rarely understood about promiscuity. In *Last Tango* there's that line "Fuck God," with which the picture begins — you can hardly hear it. Brando screams it as the Metro goes overhead. One of the profoundest motives in promiscuity and in perversion is fuck God. God, I'm defying you. A most basic human emotion. Now, whether we actually defy God when we think we do, or are unwittingly dignifying Him, even expressing His will, which has been kept from us for two thousand years — in other words, it is the pagan who expresses the will of God rather than the Christian — that we don't know. But the impulse is there.

What we can count on is that when a woman throws off her social responsibility, her tendency is to be wilder than a man. Not only in anonymous relations but in orgies. Is there anything in the literature of orgy that doesn't suggest that women are always wilder? After men are used up, the women get together. They can make love to one another for hours until the men are restored. Or maybe it's that women sit upon an endless well of sexuality, whereas men have to keep rebuilding it.

FARBAR: The opposite of orgy is marriage, I suppose. Do you feel that you are still married, in some karmic sense, or some essence of you is still married to each of your wives, and you are never away from them?

MAILER: No, but it's possible certain relations continue from one life to another. Because of a great love or a great hatred, or perhaps because they're unfulfilled.

The logic of karma, it seems to me, is that God, whatever His other motivations, may as well be considered some kind of cosmic artist, engaged in a dialogue, at the least, about the nature of existence with other cosmic artists in other parts of the universe, other gods. So the point of karma may be to enable Him to go back to certain projects, just as an artist sometimes wishes to improve his first attempt. Sometimes what an artist does is perfect. Sometimes one wants to work it further, go to the point where you can do better or, if not, know you've failed and abandon the notion. Perhaps human souls represent some of the most poignant notions of God. You see, there's an extraordinary beauty in the potential of most human relations if we're willing to assume that under all the absurdities, all the spleen and waste and brutality, there's a blocked aesthetic conception. Maybe that's why I object to some of the more casual forms of promiscuity. I don't object across the board. There are times when you need a fuck the way you need a shit. Simple as that. Let's not pretend. One of the troubles with promiscuous fucking is that you not only get the wastes out, but take in waste from the other person's system. You shit on them, and they shit on you. I think one of the best lines in *Marilyn* is, "Less is known about the true transactions of fucking than any science on earth."

FARBAR: Well then, why do so many women look upon the sex act in a much more holy way than a man does?

MAILER: They do, they don't. Some have absolute contempt for sex. Probably just as many women think of sex as evacuation as men. They enjoy sex, but despise it. One of the drives in women's lib is to insist that women are absolutely as cynical about sex as men and have the right to be absolutely as cynical.

FARBAR: Remember when the Pill first came on the scene and made a lot of young people very happy? There was a lot of screwing, and then gradually, the way it is now, there seems to be less joy in sex. When I was eighteen or twenty, I'd be screwing my brains out if it were possible.

MAILER: You were screwing your brains out because it was a criminal activity in your day, and so offered more pleasure than law-abiding activity. Which has been my argument about permissiveness in sex from the beginning. It's why I'm opposed to legalization of marijuana. Reduce the penalties, but don't have marijuana legal. The corporation will take it over. Marijuana with filter-tip cigarettes. You'll have vitamins in the marijuana, and every pollution of advertising. You'll come to hate the very thought of smoking because they'll be working their scheme on you.

By the same token, the moment you get too much permissiveness in sex, you get pulled into somebody else's manipulation scheme. My idea these years is that total promiscuity is the unstated need of the technological society. Its impulse is to accept indiscriminate fucking. It wants humans to become units. About the time we no longer distinguish between a man and a woman, he-she has become an interchangeable sexual part. We put it into the hole of those weaker than us, and get it put into our own hole by those stronger; we become a link in a technological chain of sex.

I've always hated the Pill. It reduces the fuck to a species of upper masturbation. Part of the beauty of the fuck was that you were taking a terrible chance. You could knock the girl up, and if you did, then by God you found out what you really felt about her, how phony were you, how true. When a woman comes to you and says she's pregnant, you know more about what you feel for her than you did before.

All right, the women will counter and say, That's good for you, finding your identity, but we're losing ours. Because we have to get butchered by abortionists. I've never been able to answer this. I will agree that the absence of the Pill was better for the sanity of men than women. I think women, if they are willing to look at themselves in such fashion, are in the embattled position. Since they are closer to creation, they have to pay more for the privilege. They hate it now. They hate it because we live in a technological world, where to be pregnant means that you're removed for a time from the major scene, which is to say the whole technological process. The last power of the human heart as we approach apocalypse is ambition. Everybody gets more ambitious to be in on more. If we can't wield the power, then we want to be in on the shaping of the power.

FARBAR: What about legalized abortion?

MAILER: I think when a woman goes through an abortion, even legalized abortion, she goes through hell. There's no use hoping otherwise. For what is she doing? Sometimes she has to be saying to herself, "You're killing the memory of a beautiful fuck." I don't think abortion is a great strain when the act was some miserable little screech, or some squeak oozed up through the trapdoor, a little rat which got in, a worm who slithered under the threshold. That sort of abortion costs a woman little more than discomfort. Unless there are medical consequences years later.

But if a woman has a great fuck, and then has to abort, it embitters her. A profound and awful transaction. The Pill didn't come into existence for nothing.

FARBAR: Do you see any future in a formal structure of marriage? Many young people in various strata of society are no longer getting married.

MAILER: We return to our beginning. I think marriage has a future of a sort. I think it's going to become a classical demand on people. Of course, few people are interested in classical demands. Those who are will look upon marriage with more regard than they have in a century. Because it's not going to be easy to imagine a man and woman getting married when they're young and both virgins, say at the age of eighteen or twenty or twenty-two, and then proceeding to live in happiness and fidelity for fifty or sixty years in order to die together. That is soon going to be equal in difficulty to pitching a no-hitter. And will be respected in the same fashion. The virtuosity of the demand is finally going to keep marriage alive. Not necessarily as a fundamental social institution, but as a grand curiosity. Because there will always be that human wonder. Maybe that was the way it was supposed to be. Maybe there is nothing more beautiful than one man and one woman managing to be that much to each other. What courage it takes, what extraordinary leaps, what a transcendent vision one needs of the mate. What a transcendent vision one needs of existence in order to ride out the boredom, the entrenched monotonies, the temptations, the small betrayals, the social pressures, and finally the huge social weight of that oncoming future, which will hardly encourage anyone to remain faithful, for to stay in marriage will appear absurd.

The point is you can't cheat life. Go back to Willingham's notion. You pay for everything. The worst notion afoot among the young people I know is that you can get fucking for nothing. You don't get it that way. You pay for fucking with your life and you end with your death. Then something in the balance of things may decide whether you've earned your reincarnation. The new life we're given may be the closest we ever come to the truth.

1973

One-Night Stands

An Interview with Cathleen Medwick

✢

CATHLEEN MEDWICK: What we're thinking about is an interview on love.

NORMAN MAILER: Love?

MEDWICK: Primarily.

MAILER: Oh — I don't know if I can talk about it.

MEDWICK: I know — I don't know if I can ask you.

MAILER: Let's say that I have enough respect for love so that I think if you start to talk about it, you can get into an awful lot of trouble. You're likely to let all the devils in the cosmos in on your little secret, whatever it is that enables you to trap a little of that substance that's rarer than gold. I mean, if a man had a small supply of gold, he wouldn't go around telling people where he mined it, would he? So I think that the only people who want to talk about love are those who don't have any and pretend to know something about it.

MEDWICK: The reason we're so curious is that people don't necessarily associate sex with love, and I think that you do, almost invariably.

✳ MAILER: Well I think they have a fugue-like relationship, and keep going in and out of one another.

MEDWICK: Yes. You know, I should tell you, or maybe I shouldn't, that most of the time when I read your descriptions of very intimate sex, it reads — it reminds me of something, I couldn't figure

103

out until recently what it was. And I realized that it reminded me of medieval romances that I had read as a graduate student.

MAILER: Yeah, Marion Faye at the end of *The Deer Park* when he's thinking of his relation to Elena, and I guess Rojack in *The American Dream*. Sure. That's as close as I ever came really to writing about sex. I find that in a funny way I'm slightly embarrassed by explicit descriptions. You know, I did a book about Henry Miller a few years ago and he is such a marvelous pornographic writer, that is I don't know whether he'd call himself a pornographic writer or not, and I don't want to insult the old boy, especially now that he's gone, but let's say he wrote about riproaring sex like nobody else. I really felt like a maiden aunt next to him, I'm so nice-nelly compared to Miller. I'm not sure that I really know how to write about sex. I'm always making it too metaphorical.

MEDWICK: Did you ever by any chance read anything that Saint Teresa wrote about her mystical experience?

MAILER: No.

MEDWICK: Well, she described being invaded by the spirit of God in terms that were extremely sexual by modern standards. When the nineteenth-century critics read it they thought, "My God, she thought she was talking about something spiritual but she was really talking about a complete sexual experience." It was very hard to convince them that not only was she aware that she was translating it that way but that there was no reason not to talk about it that way. Do you consider your feelings about sex and love to be somewhat mystical; romantic?

MAILER: That's why I'm not happy talking about it. If you interview a mystic, you've got the single most difficult variety of interview on your hands. Mystics feel about interviews the way primitive people feel about being photographed. It goes back to Hemingway's notion: "If it feels good, don't talk about it." One can talk around it, but I'm not going to give you a definition of love and a definition of sex. I'm going to speak guardedly and circumferentially and let readers make of it what they will in relation to their own experience. That's the way most people talk about sex and love most of the time anyway. My mother once described the plot of *Romeo and Juliet* by saying, "Well, I think they kind of liked each other," my mother having been brought up in a school which believed you should never talk about personal relationships at all.

MEDWICK: Well, do you think that men love differently than women?

MAILER: Let's try to separate sex and love. For instance, it's possible sex inspires more mystical feelings than love. I'm talking about love in the immediate sense, A loves B. Terribly concrete and particular. You love the way someone walks, the way they talk, the way they do all those things in the songs, you love the way they smell and you love the way they wear clothing, you love the way they laugh, you love the way they tell a joke, you love the way they say no to somebody — it's all the things they do. Whereas sex very often makes you feel close to God. Now if you love someone, and if you also have good sex with her, then you can feel very close to God as you love. In fact, it's easier to feel close if you have good sex with someone you love, because having good sex with somebody you don't like can leave you with an angry, confused, lustful feeling that may inspire you to more and more sex until you burn it out, and it drives you further and further away from any tenderness. To that extent you offer nothing to God, you're only thinking of the Devil. Sex also inspires, very often, a feeling that you're awfully close to the Devil. But I think the paradox of sex is that you can have sex with someone you don't know, on the first night, and feel closer to God in that moment than you're likely to feel again for five or ten years, even if you're never going to see the person again. You may say goodbye in the morning and never see each other again, a romance in the airport or something. Although I must confess I've never had a romance in an airport — can you imagine finding God in all that plastic?

MEDWICK: I'm not sure where that leaves love. How much of that feeling remains, that close-to-God feeling remains in a long-term relationship?

MAILER: Well, if one loves one's wife and loves one's children, after a while you begin to feel very close to God — not that your wife is God or the child's God but you're married to still one more aspect of the creation, whatever it is. That is, you touch God. That is the way in which most people become quietly religious, and say at the end of a period of many years, "Yes, I believe in God, I believe in God very much." There's been a quiet growth of sentiment without them necessarily thinking about it. They go along for years with their children, and at a certain point they find themself praying. Let's say a child is ill, they're praying for the child's protection and they realize they've gotten very close to God because they've seen this extraordinary miracle of a child growing every day, and changing and having some life that's just not explicable by the wife's wit or the husband's. So the creation becomes beautiful, and manifest. But as I say, that's not the way of the mystic. If you would, that's finding Christ through works.

The first time that someone has a profound sexual act, when it's all over, there's this shocked, stunned, incredible recognition: "Why God, God exists." Which is what Saint Teresa felt perhaps. I say it usually happens in sex rather than in love because it's got to happen quickly, a sudden revelation. So there are certain advantages to one-night stands. One brings none of one's baggage to a one-night stand and that makes it possible to have, once in a while, extraordinary emotions. The average one-night stand is, after all, not necessarily a small disaster, but unless it's very, very good indeed it leaves a terrible aftertaste. They can be exceptional once in a while; when that happens one often has this religious sentiment. It doesn't come from the person — you don't know the person — it comes from something in sex itself. Sex may be something that's outside of people.

MEDWICK: I can't seem to think of a woman who has written about sex in this way, or love in this way. I can think of five or six men.

MAILER: I would argue that women have an immense horror of exposing themselves. Let me give an example. When I wrote *An American Dream*, many people were offended profoundly by the sexual act that takes place between the hero Rojack and the German maid Ruta. It would have been impossible — if Ruta, and not Rojack, had been telling the story — for her to write about that act without revealing herself completely, and in a disadvantageous way. The man could write about it, because one-night stands are altogether different from a continuing sexual relationship where the man dominates in one way, the woman dominates in another, they share here, they're apart there, and it changes over a period of time. In the one-night stand there was, at least until very recently, the notion that no matter what they did in bed, the man was dominant in that he had scored the breakthrough and the woman had been taken, at least in the eyes of society.

MEDWICK: Is that changing now, do you think?

MAILER: Oh, a great deal. It's almost getting to the point where women are saying, "*I* scored."

MEDWICK: What does that do to the mythology?

MAILER: Well, I don't think one generation can wipe out what may or may not be biological and is certainly historical. But a woman is not going to admit as readily as a man that she had an extraordinary experience on a one-night stand. Ten or twenty years ago you'd hear of a woman who slashed her wrists — often what happened was that she had an extraordinary experience with a man she met for a night and never heard from again, and that made her feel she was crazy or evil or didn't deserve to live. I'm not saying that one-night stands are better than living in considerable sexual intensity with someone for a long time. I'm not saying that at all. I'm saying that it can be hard for the long-term relationship to be mystical. One reaches heights from time to time, and in fact one may go higher and further with someone one knows very well than one could ever go on a one-night stand, but since a one-night stand is often transcendental to the degree that you really don't know the other person, that they are *strange* — like the cosmos — it suggests that when you're living with someone you love, sex can't be transcendental in that particular way at all. Of course it gets its richness in other ways, but we've talked of that.

1980

Ethics and Pornography

An Interview with Jeffrey Michelson and Sarah Stone

❧

JEFFREY MICHELSON: What do you think makes for great sex?

NORMAN MAILER: Great sex is apocalyptic. There's no such thing as great sex unless you have an apocalyptic moment. William Burroughs once changed the course of American literature with one sentence. He said, "I see God in my asshole in the flashbulb of orgasm."* Now that was one incredible sentence because it came at the end of the Eisenhower period, printed around 1959 in *Big Table* in Chicago. I remember reading it and thinking, "I can't believe I just read those words." I can't tell you the number of taboos it violated. First of all, you weren't supposed to connect God with sex. Second of all, you never spoke of the asshole, certainly not in relation to sex. If you did, you were the lowest form of pervert. Third of all, there was obvious homosexuality in the remark. In those days, nobody was accustomed to seeing that in print. And fourth, there was an ugly technological edge — why'd he have to bring in flashbulbs? Was that the nature of his orgasm? It was the first time anybody had ever spoken about the inner nature of the orgasm.

MICHELSON: Yeah.

MAILER: OK. Looking at it now, that marvelously innovative sentence, with all it did, one of the most explosive sentences ever written in the English language, we can take off from it and say that unless sex is apocalyptic, we can't speak of it as great. We can

---

* The first sentence in *Naked Lunch* as it was printed in *Big Table*.

speak of it as resonant. We can speak of it as heart-warming. We can speak of it as lovely. But we can't speak of it as great. Great is a word that should never be thrown around in relation to sex. My simple belief is that sex that makes you more religious is great sex. I'm going to live to pay for, to rue, this remark if it gets around.

MICHELSON: I'll never tell anyone. (*laughter*)

MAILER: Remember that awful priest who said, "There are no atheists in foxholes?" It was a remark to turn people into atheists for twenty-five years. I remember every time I got into a foxhole I said to myself, "This is one man who's an atheist in a foxhole!" (*laughter*) Well, what I do believe is that you can't have a great fuck and remain an atheist. Now that means the atheists of America are going to excoriate me. This is striking at them; this is a true blow at their sexual happiness.

MICHELSON: What is the relationship between God and sex, and the Devil and sex?

MAILER: You can't talk about it that way.

MICHELSON: Tell me about the orgies you went to when you were younger?

MAILER: I'm not going to tell you. Certain things belong to my novels. Look, let me make one thing clear: there are matters I won't talk about in an interview. Anything I would find tremendously difficult to write about in a novel, I'm not going to try to discuss in an interview. If it can't be done in a novel, it certainly can't be done here.

MICHELSON: Did you go to one orgy as a philosopher, or did you go to many as a pervert?

MAILER: You're referring to Voltaire's little remark, "Once a philosopher, twice a pervert." Voltaire went once to a male brothel and his friends asked him afterward did he like it, and he said, "Oh, yes, very much. It was better than I thought it would be." They said, "Are you going back?" and he said, "No. Once a philosopher, twice a pervert." Well, I'm not going to tell you.

MICHELSON: I would like to get on to your feelings about sexuality. Not to intrude on your own life, but just to discuss certain things. What do you think you know about sex that most other people do not?

MAILER: Jeffrey, I can't possibly answer that. I'd have to believe it's true . . . Really, all I believe is that I'm more aware of my limitations than most men. I have less vanity about sex than most men.

MICHELSON: You've grown to have less vanity?

MAILER: Yeah. I used to have an immense amount when I was younger. I needed it. I had an immense amount to learn. Sexual vanity probably has an inverse proportion to sexual sophistication. When we're young, we have to believe we're the greatest gift given to women because if we didn't, we would know how truly bad we are. When I was a kid, I remember I had an older cousin who was immensely successful with women. And I was always obsessed with performance. He used to say to me, "You're wrong on that; performance has nothing to do with it." I never knew what he meant. It took years — he was considerably older than me — to come to understand what he was talking about. Performance is empty in sex. Performance is pushups. I mean, we've all had the experience of making love for hours, and getting that airless, tight, exhausted feeling, you know, my God, will she ever come? For God's sakes, please, God, please, let her come! (*laughter*) I have a bad back today and one of the reasons is that I worked so hard when I was younger.

MICHELSON: At sex?

MAILER: I didn't work at lifting furniture, I promise you. If I'd been a furniture mover, at least I'd have some honor. (*laughter*) No, I have a bad back because I was stupid. Because I tried to ... you see, the minute you try to dominate sex through will, sex escapes you. The connection of female sexuality with cats is not for too little. You cannot dominate a cat with your will. If you do, the cat goes right around you. Sexuality is the same way: can't dominate it. So over the years as you come to recognize this, you begin to approach it from the side, so to speak.

MICHELSON: Tell me about your first experience with pornography. Do you remember when you were a kid and the first magazines you had?

MAILER: I think it was *Spicy Detective*.

MICHELSON: *Spicy Detective*?

MAILER: There used to be magazines called *Spicy Detective* and *Spicy* — I can't remember the others, maybe *Spicy Romance*. The girls always had marvelous large breasts, with tremendously pointed nipples. I don't know how to describe these breasts, it almost fails me. You couldn't call them pear-shaped, nor melon-shaped, somewhere in between. They were projectile-shaped. Literally, they looked like the head of a 105 Howitzer shell, about 4 inches in diameter, and went out about 5½ inches, with those tremendously pointed nipples. The girl always used to be tied to some sort of hitching post with an evil man approaching. They always had one arm under their breasts. I remember that it made the breasts project out even more. They'd have a wisp of clothing. A torn panty would cover their loins. I've never seen anything I enjoyed as much. Now, I didn't learn much from it.

MICHELSON: Do you feel that there are any social benefits that result from a sexually free press, or do you feel that sexually explicit material must be tolerated simply to protect the wider benefits of the First Amendment?

MAILER: Well, the first benefit is sexual sophistication. Talk about pornography always revolves around: Does it excite more violent impulses, or doesn't it? The women's movement is absolutely up in arms about pornography. An encouragement to rape, et cetera. I just can't agree. I think they don't know quite what they're talking about. Of course, some kinds of pornography are on the cusp. I wouldn't have anything to say for pornography that uses children as models. I'm against anything that sets people's lives on certain tracks too early. Using a child to make money from sex is obviously offensive. If you were a magazine that had pictures of children performing sexual acts, I wouldn't be in it. That's where I draw the line.

But you asked what the social value might be. Pictures of men and women making love is not going to hurt people as much as it's going to help them. It gives them — and I would include pornographic movies — an education in that part of sex which is universal, as opposed to the part that's particular. Those tragedies of high school kids who get married too young, only to discover three, five, eight years later, with a couple of children between them, that they weren't meant for one another at all, and so split, come about because the sex is so compelling when they're young and they know so little about it. That's a profound error we've all made one way or another. We mistake the beauties of sex for the beauties of the particular person that we're with, that is, think the particular person is beautiful because of the sexual feelings they arouse in us. We don't understand those feelings are more or less universal, and could be felt with someone else. The faculty of choice is not present. Now when I was a kid, and I've never known a kid who wasn't absolutely riveted by pornography, I wanted more and more of it. I never saw enough of it to satisfy myself. That's because there's tremendous knowledge there, tremendous knowledge about human behavior. You cannot look at a pornographic picture without learning more about human nature. I can look at some girl who has, on the face of it, a stupid face, let's say — some of the girls who appear in pornographic magazines look stupid, some rather bright. But let's take one that looks stupid. Nevertheless, there's something in the very way she holds her hand (even if the photographer arranged her hand for her, she had finally to embody his order) there's something in the way her hand is holding a cigarette that'll tell you a great deal about her if you look carefully enough at these matters.

You also get a sense of the sexual behavior of a panorama of people that you couldn't possibly have in your own life unless you devoted your life to sex. One of the ironies of pornography is that it enables people to free themselves from chasing after sex. A lot of that knowledge can now be obtained in a secondary fashion, through pornography.

MICHELSON: Knowledge as opposed to pleasure?

MAILER: Yes. If we all had to go out and acquire every bit of understanding through our own experience, it would take us forever to learn anything. That's why, in fact, civilization moved so slowly for so many thousands of years. From Gutenberg on, there's been an incredible rate of acceleration. Now, people were able to acquire most of their knowledge by reading. They didn't have to go through the experience themselves. The worst thing you can say against pornography, I mean, the only argument I would use if I were determined to stamp pornography out is that it tends to accelerate the same things that are being speeded up by all other communications. Pornography, right at this present point, is a peculiar frontier of communications.

SARAH STONE: What exactly is accelerated?

MAILER: The consciousness of people. In the simplest literal sense, a kid of eighteen will now know what he wouldn't have known till he was twenty-eight.

STONE: Why is that against pornography?

MAILER: Well, if you say that everything is speeding up too quickly and we may end up destroying ourselves because we're advancing at too great a rate and don't really know what we're doing, then, in that sense, pornography is dangerous. But by the same measure, television is endlessly more dangerous. Conservatives who believe that human nature should be slowed up have a legitimate argument, I'd say, against pornography. But they're not consistent. Because if this is their argument against pornography, let them ban television first.

MICHELSON: Do you feel comfortable about appearing in *Puritan*?

MAILER: Not altogether. I've thought about it, and finally decided I probably ought to. I'm not opposed to pornography — in fact, I think it probably has a social benefit. On the other hand, in *Playboy* I've had the experience of seeing my work printed between beaver shots. Now, *Playboy* happens to treat its writers exceptionally well. No magazine is nicer in terms of courtesy, and you get fine pay for your stuff. They're a godawful magazine, however, in terms of layout, at least from the point of view of the writer, because the last thing you want for your prose, is to have a photo of a gorgeous model with her legs going from Valparaiso to Baltimore! Right in the middle of your prose! I'd rather you took an axe and drove it into the middle of the reader's head. Because the reader's not going to follow my stuff. His eye is on the bird. So there have been times when, despite the attractions of *Playboy*, I don't really want that piece there. It's not going to be read properly. In that sense, pornography is a tremendous distraction for a writer.

MICHELSON: I'll try to make sure the layout keeps all your words together.

MAILER: At least let me pick the pictures.

MICHELSON: When does a graphic representation of a sexual act become art, and when, smut? Can you suggest any criteria on which to base a judgment?

MAILER: Let me ask you: what would be *your* idea of smut?

MICHELSON: Things that are particularly degrading to either sex.

MAILER: Get specific.

MICHELSON: I guess it's stuff that turns me on in a way I think I shouldn't be turned on.

MAILER: Excellent.

STONE: I feel the difference is if it's commercially and sloppily done just to get another page in the book, then the insult is to the art. Where it's a true and honest representation of feeling, then no matter what it represents, it's got to be respected.

MAILER: Mmm, that's well put too. You would be saying in effect, then, Sarah, that smut is the equivalent of a sexual act that's casual, what we call sordid, no love, not any real pleasure in it, a cohabitation with a rancid smell to it. So a lack of respect for the seriousness of the occasion when a photographer takes a picture of a woman in a pornographic position makes for smut.

Jeffrey is saying, as I gather, that there are certain acts that tend toward the bestial, the fecal (I assume these are the sort of things you're thinking of) that may be arousing, but you find that your moral nature disapproves.

MICHELSON: I'm wondering: Is smut to pornography, to good pornography, as trashy romance novels are to good literature? Is it just the lower end of the genre?

MAILER: It's certainly complicated. Take Sarah's criteria, pictures that are transparently cynical. The model's worn out, the photographer's worn out, disgusting. Yet that can be arousing in a funny way. For instance, in *Hustler*, often I find that the most interesting section is those cheap Polaroid pictures that untalented photographers send in of women who are not professional models.

MICHELSON: The reality turns you on?

MAILER: The sordid reality. My sexuality, I expect, is aroused by knowledge. The moment I know more than I knew before, I'm excited. Those gritty Polaroid shots in *Hustler* are often more interesting. They communicate. You know, the picture of some waitress who lives in Sioux Falls. I know more at that moment about Sioux Falls, about waitresses — even if they're lying, even if she isn't a waitress, there's something about the very manifest of the lie that's presented that's fascinating. It arouses your curiosity. Whereas superb pictures of models can get boring. There tends to be a sameness to them. Aren't enough flaws present. The very question of the sordid is . . . tricky.

STONE: In Woody Allen's movie *Annie Hall*, he's on the street and he walks up to this little old lady and says to her something like "Why are relationships so difficult?" And she says, "Love fades . . ." As a man who's had six marriages, what is your reaction to this dialogue? Do you think that love fades and do you feel that sex fades?

MAILER: I don't think that sex fades in marriage necessarily. Without talking about my personal life, I'd say that compatibility is nearer to the problem than sex. What I mean is people can have marvelous sex and not be terribly compatible. That sets up a great edginess in marriage. Some people, in fact, can only have good sex with people who are essentially incompatible for them. I might have been in that category for years, I don't know. If you're terribly combative, then you're drawn toward mates who are not too compatible. Anyone who has a violent or ugly or combative edge is not going to be comfortable with someone who *is* really sweet and submissive. They want something more abrasive in their daily life. Otherwise they are likely to lose their good opinion of themselves. There's nothing worse than being brutal to somebody who's good to you. Whereas if you're living with someone whose ideas irritate the living shit out of you, and you fight with them every day and feel justified about it, that can be healthier than living with a soul whose ideas are compatible to yours. All the same, if you do choose this fundamental imcompatibility, there will come a point where it ceases to be fun and turns into its opposite. Faults in the mate that were half-charming suddenly become unendurable. Every one of us who has been in love knows how fragile — what's a good word for skin? — how fragile is the *membrane* of love. It has to be mended every day and nurtured. We have to anticipate all the places where it's getting a little weak and go there and breathe on it, shape it again. In a combative relationship, obviously, that's difficult. You have to have a great animal vigor between combative people or they just can't make it for long.

MICHELSON: What about love fading?

MAILER: Well, I don't think love fades; I don't think there's anything automatic about it. I think most of us aren't good enough for love. I think self-pity is probably the most rewarding single emotion in the world for masturbators, which is one of the reasons, I suppose, I'm opposed to masturbation, because it encourages other vices to collect around you. Self-pity is one of the first. You lie in bed, pull off, and say to yourself, I have such wonderful, beautiful, tender, sweet, deep, romantic, exciting and sensual emotions, why is it that no woman can appreciate how absolutely fabulous I am? Why can't I offer these emotions to someone else? Self-pity comes rolling in, and cuts us off from recognizing that love is a reward. Love is not something that is going to come up and solve your problems. Love is something you get after you've solved enough of your problems so that something in Providence itself takes pity on you. I always believed that whoever or whatever it is, some angel, some sour sort of angel, finally says, "Look at those poor motherfuckers. He and she have been working so hard for so many years. Let's throw him and her a bone." So they meet and find love. Then they have to know what to do with it.

MICHELSON: Love is a function of having paid your dues?

MAILER: Truman Capote has got this book he's writing, *Answered Prayers*. I gather from something he said once that its theme is that the worst thing that befalls people is that their prayers are answered. Which is not a cheap idea. Love is the perfect example. Everybody prays for love, but once they get love, they have to be worthy of it. Love is the most perishable of human emotions. It never fades. That's my answer to the question. There is absolutely no reason in the world why people can't love each other more every day of their lives for eighty years. I absolutely believe that. Without that, I have no faith in love whatsoever. I think it would be a diabolical universe if you're introduced to all these wonderful sentiments that illumine your existence but something is put into the very nature of it that will make it fade. That's the sentiment of a person who is full of self-pity: Love fades. That old woman was full of self-pity.

MICHELSON: Do you feel that there is a spiritual obligation to sexual relationships, and if so, what price do we pay if we don't live up to it?

MAILER: Well, it's always a spiritual obligation. But the trouble with the word spiritual is that we think of churches and priests and clergymen. I do think there's a spiritual demand in love, however, more a demand than an obligation. Love asks that we be a little braver than is comfortable for us, a little more generous, a little more flexible. It means living on the edge more than we care to. Love is always in danger of being the most painful single emotion we can ever feel, other than perhaps a sudden knowledge of our own death. La Rochefoucauld has that wonderful remark that half the people in the world would never have fallen in love if they had not heard of the word. I think that most people I know, maybe three-quarters of the people I know, have never been deeply in love.

MICHELSON: Talking about not being deeply in love, have you ever paid for sex, and what is your opinion about hookers and johns and the outright exchange of sex for money?

MAILER: Well, take it at its best. Because at its worst, there is nothing worse than paying for sex, and being thrown a bad, cynical, dull fuck by a whore who either has no talent, or no interest in you, or feels you don't deserve anything better than you are getting. That's one of the worst single experiences there is. On balance, counting the number of times I've had good sex in whorehouses and bad, I could almost do without it. But, you know, living fifty-eight years, you end up with a lot of experiences. I've had a few extraordinary times in whorehouses, which I'll have to write about some day, too. So I wouldn't put it down altogether. It's just that it's immensely more difficult, I think, to have good sex with a whore unless you're oriented that way.

There are a lot of guys who are not homosexual, but grow up in a male environment. They have four brothers, or they're jocks, or just live in a male environment as so many smalltown kids do. They're less comfortable with women, and so if all their buddies have been plowing the same broad — and I use these two words, "plowing" and "broad" because that's the way they're looking at it; they're really looking upon it as a field — the fact that they're going to be mixing their semen with the effluvia of their buddies is tremendously aphrodisiacal to them. So sex can be intense for men in whorehouses. It doesn't mean that they're homosexual; that's too quick a jump to make. What it does mean is that they have to cut that close to the edges of homosexual experience in order to get a real send-off.

MICHELSON: You said to Buzz Farbar in a *Viva* interview that you couldn't afford to begin — this is a quote, you "couldn't afford to begin to get homosexual because God knows where it'd stop." Do you feel that homosexual impulses should be repressed, and quite candidly, have you ever experienced such impulses?

MAILER: I've never experienced them dramatically. I've never ever said, "Oh, I got to have that boy," or "I've got to go to bed with that man." I feel it's been a buried theme in my life but a powerful one. It creates its presence by its absence. I don't think you can be an artist without having a . . . well, let's try to define the elements a little.

There are homosexuals who have essentially male experience and others who have female. In a funny way, the difference between male and female in homosexuality is more marked, probably, than it is between men and women. When a man and a woman make love, they can take turns: one more aggressive, then the other — there are many ways in which a woman can almost literally fuck a man. The woman can be active, the man passive, then they reverse it. Many good sexual relationships consist of that back and forth. Nothing like the dialectic when you get down to it. But, in male sexuality, there is a tendency to either be top or bottom, back or front. They have an expression: Did you do it or were you done to? There is much more identification with whether you're going to be the male or the female in the relationship.

Now, I think all humans are born with a man and a woman in us. I think that's self-evident: we have a mother and a father, and to the degree that the mother is female and male both, we have a female-male component in ourselves. In turn, through our fathers we have a male-female side to ourselves. At the least, two sexual systems within us, psychically, at any rate. I also suspect male artists have more of a female component to their nature than the average male. I think that's why I've always stayed away from homosexuality. I suppose I felt the female side of my nature would have been taken over by homosexuality to a degree that would have been repulsive to me. What you get down to is that it's a man who's doing it to you. And the man in me does not wish to be dominated by another man, not that way, not that way.

Now the homosexuals whose masculinity comes out through homosexuality are very proud of themselves. I mean, those homosexuals will say, "We're more men than the average heterosexual. The average heterosexual makes love to a woman who is physically weaker than himself. But we men, we go out and we stick it in the asses of men who can fight back, we're real men." In prison, there's great pride in who's doing it to who, because finally what you may be doing is putting it up the ass of a killer — which would give me pause, I'll tell you that. So, when I was younger, I used to cover all these feelings by feeling antipathy toward homosexuals. I don't feel that now. I just think all that is not for me. Any more than becoming a Hindu fakir would be a way of life for me, or going down at the age of fifty-eight to Texas to work in the oil wells, that wouldn't really be a reasonable life any longer.

MICHELSON: A friend of mine who grew up in Puerto Rico said that there the onus is only on the catcher, not the pitcher. Puerto Ricans, he said, didn't consider people who fucked people in the ass homosexuals. They only considered people who got fucked in the ass homosexuals. So that's just a cultural bias.

MAILER: Didn't I say earlier that the difference between the male and female sides of homosexuality is greater than the male and female aspects of heterosexuality?

MICHELSON: As long as the Puerto Rican was in the male role, he was still a male.

MAILER: Certainly criminals, and ghetto people, and tough ethnics do have that attitude, there's no question to it. To some men, active homosexuality doesn't hurt their masculinity; it reinforces it from their point of view.

One thing on which I have a bugaboo is that Women's Liberation keeps talking about rape, rape, rape. So far as I can make out, more men are probably raped every year than women, at least when you get into true cases of rape where it's absolutely against your will. I'll grant that there are many marginal cases of rape between men and women, where the woman rather likes the guy, but doesn't want to do it tonight, and the guy insists, and lo and behold, she ends up doing it tonight. But that's much nearer to lack of moral consent than rape. Women's Lib throws all those cases into rape. If you only count cases of true force, where there's absolutely no desire on the one hand, and absolute determination on the other hand, I'm willing to bet there are more cases of male rape every year than female rape. Because in the prisons, thousands of men are done to every year.

MICHELSON: I know you're now to the right of the Pope on masturbation. But in the past, have you ever masturbated to an erotic photograph?

MAILER: Of course. In adolescence.

MICHELSON: Why have you become so puritanical about masturbation?

MAILER: I'm not puritanical about it. Puritans put people in jail for their activities, or bring social censure against them. I don't go out with a flag and walk it up and down outside certain people's houses . . .

MICHELSON: Ban masturbation!

MAILER: . . . but, God, I happen to believe, just like the nineteenth-century preachers, that the ultimate tendency of masturbation is insanity.

MICHELSON: You think it does lead to insanity?

MAILER: Well, it doesn't lead to it instantly. People can jerk off all their lives and they're not going to go insane. I said the *ultimate tendency* of masturbation is insanity. Now the ultimate tendency of driving a car at 80 miles an hour in a 55-mile-an-hour zone is collision. But there are people who drive at 80 miles an hour until the cops stop them or indeed, never get caught, but neither do they collide. The ultimate tendency remains just that. My point, however, is that left to itself masturbation does not bring you back into the world, it drives you further out of the world. You don't have the objective correlative.

You see, one of the arguments I would bring against pornography, especially the pornography of my adolescence, is that it encourages fantasy and romance. If I had a fault to find with the pornography magazines in general, it would be that they tend to satisfy elements of fantasy and romance. In other words, they don't — let me see if I can find some analogy. If a kid dreams about football as a wonderful game where he is running for touchdowns, and that's all he ever visualizes, he'd have a rude shock, to say the least, the first time he got into an actual game, was dumped hard and had a headache afterward. There's nothing like the first tackle or block you throw to wake you up to one fact: If you're going to love football, you have to love it *with* its punishment. And at that point, loving it that way, you have a profound relation to football. To love with the full awareness of punishment is the nature of profundity. So, to the degree that pornography encourages people to believe that sex is easy, it's harmful. But I can't see this as a social harm, since everything in the scheme of things encourages us to believe that life is easier than it is.

One of the fundamental tenets of this business of selling America, selling modern life, is to present modern life as *nicer* than it is. As an example, you have these ads that show the happiness of dishwashing machines. Well, the nearest I came to have a major fight with my wife was the other night, she'd bought a new dishwasher and the thing smelled of plastic. It had the most hideous smell, that kind of antiseptic odor insane people douse themselves with. You know how certain insane people put sort of an antiseptic perfume on themselves. Ever smell that? That damn dishwasher smelled that way. I went into a rage. I said, "You've just bought part of the grand American scheme to drive us out of the kitchen. This thing stinks so bad that you'll never spend time cooking anything."

STONE: It smelled because it was new?

MAILER: That's what she claimed. But I'm telling you that smell's never going to go away. They're putting the odor in so people will go out and buy TV dinners. That's part of the scheme. That's what McDonald's, superhighways, and all general plastic crap is all about. Everything in the scheme of things drives us toward living in a way we don't want to live.

Pornography, to the degree it's sentimental and romantic, is fudging the issue too, not increasing knowledge, but muddying knowledge.

MICHELSON: Are you against fantasy?

MAILER: Against sentimental fantasy. That, I think, is our introduction to cancer. A ticket to the gulch.

STONE: What sexual fantasies get you hot?

MAILER: I won't get into it for a variety of reasons. Years ago a friend of mine agreed to fill out a sexual questionnaire. He had to go through every girl he'd laid, describe her in detail, what they did, their fantasies, their water sports. After he was finished, for the first time in his life (and this kid was a stud) he was impotent for three months. So one holds onto one's little fantasies.

Actually, I have very few left at this point. As you get older, you need fantasy less and less. Let me put it this way: Fantasy gives resonance to sex so long as it's on the threshold of reality. If two people are making love and play a little game, and pretend they're other people, well, that's perfectly all right. Finally they have to do the acting job. It's not just simple fantasy. But if a man and woman are making love, and the man secretly thinks that he is fucking the Countess Eloise of Bulgaria, and the woman is visualizing a stud from Harlem for herself, then they're in trouble whether they know it or not. Essentially they are masturbating. The ultimate tendency of such love-making is insanity.

MICHELSON: Upper masturbation.

STONE: Then what sexual realities get you hot?

MAILER: Nothing remarkable about it. The innermost parts of the female body exposed, that gets me hot. A fine pair of breasts, a beautiful ass. Hands can get me, not hot, but started. I mean, some women have beautiful hands. It's really not important. To find a woman attractive there has to be some one feature that truly keeps pulling you back. It could be her face, her hands, it could be her toes — you don't have to be a shrimper to love a woman's feet, because it isn't literally the hands or the feet that turn you on. A certain statement about the private nature of that woman's sexuality is in the part of the body that excites you. A breast could be adventurous. That would excite certain men. Others might like a breast that's very domesticated, I mean, men that want to dominate a household are not going to be turned on by a breast that's adventurous. It may turn them on, but it's not going to bring them back again and again 'cause such a breast means trouble to them. Brings out their violent impulses. On the contrary, if they find a woman who's got a gentle, domesticated breast, that'll turn them on because it means they can dominate that woman. And so forth. You can go through the various parts of the body. Every body, in effect, presents a possible lock to our key.

STONE: How can a breast look adventurous?

MAILER: It can suggest that it would be unfaithful to you unless you're very good indeed. (*laughter*)

STONE: Why do you think physical beauty plays such an important part in men's attraction to women, and why does it play such a lesser role in women's attraction toward men?

MAILER: Well, because beauty, finally, is a scalp, no getting around it. When a man goes out with a beautiful woman, he's more respected in the world. I can remember a few ugly women who were attractive to me. Ugliness can be sexually exciting . . . But I will say that I wasn't very happy to be seen in the world with those women. You could say that was demonstrably unfair to them.

Except I'm going to stick at this liberal point. I think there may be — and here we enter into waters that are much too deep for all of us — but it may be that beauty and ugliness are karmic. One reason people are so drawn to beauty is that it speaks of healthy karma, whereas ugliness suggests debts in previous lives that were too hideous to be paid in those lives. So the penalty is worn on the face in this life. Which is why ugly people have such a rage toward God at their ugliness.

MICHELSON: But still, it's much more important for a man to have a beautiful woman than it is for a woman to have a beautiful man.

MAILER: Yeah.

MICHELSON: Please explain the nature of the inequity.

MAILER: Well, I think if you believe, as the more radical Women's Liberationists believe, that the only difference between the sexes is an extra six to eight inches of male skin in a certain place, then it just seems vastly unfair and unnatural. But I happen to believe in the asymmetry of the sexes. The only equality of the sexes comes, I would say, out of the rough balance. Women are strong here, men there. That doesn't mean we can't agree on anything, or that women are not entitled to equality in a thousand ways they do not have it now. Women's Liberationists are not wrong when they say that women've been treated unfairly for centuries. They're right. But that doesn't mean that we're alike.

MICHELSON: Apples and oranges?

MAILER: Apples and oranges are entitled to the same treatment when they're presented to the consumer. But they are still apples and oranges, not one big oraple. Presumably, men and women are entitled to the same treatment before they enter eternity.

MICHELSON: How do you feel about your sexual generation, those people who came of age sexually when you did?

MAILER: We had kind of a nice generation if you're going to look at it from the point of view of sexuality. We were all pioneers. We saw ourselves as breaking ground, as sexually liberated. One of the things that appalls me about Women's Liberation is the way they feel they discovered it. I remember my first wife was tremendously taken with the ideas of Simone de Beauvoir back in 1950. She spent an unproductive year trying to write a book which in effect would have been a precursor of Women's Liberation. She was a Women's Liberationist; I lived with a premature Women's Liberationist.

MICHELSON: Your first marriage.

MAILER: Yes. And one reason our marriage finally broke up was on precisely that. She was a very strong woman. She profoundly resented the female role into which my success had thrust her. You see, when we married, she was, if anything, stronger than me. She was perfectly prepared to go out and work for years in order to make enough money for me to stay at home and write a good many books. And if that happened, we probably would have been a happy couple of that sort, she the strong one, I the gentle one. Then what happened? I become successful so suddenly I got much more macho. My God, nothing like success for increasing the size of your muscle! I literally went from 140 to 180 pounds in one year — it wasn't all fat, it was muscle. I suddenly felt like a strong man. That altered everything between us.

STONE: There is a certain anger I've encountered with friends of mine when I've said that I know you. You approached this anger in *Prisoner of Sex*. I was wondering if you've discovered whether some of their feelings are based on something real?

MAILER: More and more I think the reason they feel this antipathy toward me is not because I am a conventional sexist. Anyone who reads this interview can see this. I don't have simple notions of machismo or anything of that sort — I think the reason is that my ideas about sexuality are more complicated than theirs, and they hate that. They have a very simple idea of sexuality and they want to ram it through. As far as I'm concerned, when they get like that, they're worse than the Communists I used to know in the '40s and '50s. I mean they are totalitarian in this aspect. They do not want deviation from their view of life. Now the only way you can ever learn anything is by deviation from your own point of view of life. You encounter it, you argue with it, you grapple with it, you're convinced by it or you convince it, and you move on.

MICHELSON: You feel like you're dealing with people with blind prejudice?

MAILER: Well, worse. I'm dealing with people with militant prejudice.

MICHELSON: Norman, I'd like to discuss the nature of inhibition, something that interests me. To put it bluntly, why is it that some women like to get fucked in the ass and some women find it distasteful? Some women like to suck cocks, some women don't. It surely is not purely physical.

MAILER: You can't talk about it generally, you just can't. Everything we do sexually is as characteristic of us as our features. The question you ask is truly bottomless. You could say to me, why do some people have noses with an overhang, and why do some tilt up? Why do we respond to these noses in different ways? I could give an answer; I mean, a nose that tilts up often suggests optimism, confidence about the future, fearlessness, but a nose that turns over suggests a certain pessimism about the very shape of things, an attachment to sentiments of doom. You have to ask next: What is the nature of form? Why do curves do these things to us? But in sexuality, you also have to ask which period of one's life are we talking about? Anyone who's lived with a woman for a few years learns that a woman's tastes can change as much as a man's. There are women who detest being fucked in the ass, as you put it — you see, I refuse to use those words myself . . . The woman who wants nothing to do with a phallus in her crack one year is turned on immensely by it another year. I will make one general observation: It's very dangerous to stick it up a woman's ass. It tends to make them more promiscuous. I'll leave that with your readers. They can think about it from their own experience. They can test it out. Those who are scientifically inclined can immediately approach their mate and tool her, if they're able. Then they can observe what happens, watch her at parties, get a private detective, check up on her. So I guess I answered your question: A woman doesn't want it up the ass because she's doing her best to be faithful to that dull pup she's got for a man, and she knows if it blasts into the center of her stubbornness, that's the end of it. She won't be able to hold onto fidelity any longer. That's one explanation. It doesn't have to be true. But you might ponder it.

MICHELSON: Have you ever been surprised by a woman because she seemed very proper outside and then was very wild in bed? Or a wild woman on the outside and still wild in bed? Is there a relationship between inhibition and personality?

MAILER: No royal road to success. (*laughter*) I'm not sure that women have a sexual nature as such. I mean, think of the variation in sexual performance — to go back to that word — you've had over your life. I'm sure you haven't been the same with all women, better with some than others, obviously. With women, I think such changes are even greater. When I was a kid in Brooklyn, we'd walk around muttering, "Ah, she's a lousy lay." You know, sure, she was a lousy lay for A, B, C, and D, then E came along. And she was so good, he couldn't even talk about it.

MICHELSON: Let me ask you your thoughts about Plato's Retreat and other on-premise swing clubs. I don't know whether you've been or not, but you certainly know what it's about. This type of anonymous sexual expression was once exclusively the province of the gay community. Does it mean anything that it's filtered into the heterosexual community? That you can go, on any given night, with your wife and these places are full of friendly people from Queens, Long Island — you know, regular, human people are going there and having their —

MAILER: Regular human people as opposed to what?

MICHELSON: People with unconventional lifestyles.

MAILER: People with conventional lives very often are tremendously drawn to orgiastic sex. That's their artistic expression. That's the way in which they are fighting society.

See, I think if there's any guarantee to America, and I believe there is (I hate to say it because it's used so cheaply by all those people who keep shouting, "Our great America, our great democracy") but I think there may be a greatness to democracy. It rests in the profound wisdom that a society can't expand unless, implicit in it, is the acceptance that people are busy working overtime to destroy the society. By that logic, democracy is more dialectical than Soviet Communism. What we recognize is that if you have a society, then you need people who are working to destroy that society. Out of the war comes a metamorphosis, which ideally will be more adaptive to the nature of a changing historical reality than more totalitarian, monolithic states. So — as I say — one natural, normal, healthy function of people is to fight society. The way in which conventional people often do it is through orgiastic behavior. I mean, Saturday night they have a ball with their friends, who either live next door in the next ranch house, or they drive 300 miles to see some other swinging couple. On Sunday they all go to church together. And they're giggling a little. They're living two lives at once. They were having that ball last night, the four of them, now they're in church together. And nobody's going to know. Some people can only feel a sense of balance and satisfaction, happiness, I might say, if they're living two lives at once. Orgiastic life provides that. Orgiastic life provides a lot of solutions for people. But it is sheer hell for people who are deeply in love. It's almost impossible, I think, to have much orgiastic life if you're profoundly in love with a woman. You can do it, but it takes the edginess in love, and absolutely exacerbates it.

MICHELSON: You've spoken about something totalitarian in people who were proselytizing orgies.

MAILER: The moment there's an attempt to make anything a panacea, then it's totalitarian. Panacea suggests that there's one way to do it. So does totalitarianism suggest that there's only one way. But the cosmos was designed by some divine intelligence who foresaw that if there was only one way to do it, everybody would go there. The world would quickly tip out of balance.

STONE: Have you been sexually pursued by literary groupies? What's it like being fucked as an image rather than a person?

MAILER: Well, I've usually been drawn to women who aren't necessarily that interested in my work. My present wife had read one book of mine before we met. She hardly knew anything about me. It's probably analogous to the poor young rich girl, who wants to be loved for herself and not her money, remember all those movies?

MICHELSON: Sure.

MAILER: You definitely don't want to be loved for your literary fame because you know more about it than anyone else and you know that literary fame has very little to do with your daily habits. I mean, finally you're an animal who lives in a den and goes around, and finally, you know, has to be liked or disliked as an animal first.

STONE: Is jealousy a necessary part of an intense sexual relationship or do you feel that it's a disease?

MAILER: It's a very good question until you realize that you can't answer it. Because you end up with platitudes. It's my general experience that if you don't feel any jealousy at all, a woman will have profound doubt of your love. A little jealousy is marvelously aphrodisiacal, you know that, but real jealousy, when it takes over, is delusional, and has all the dirty pleasures of delusion. Delusion is one of the most profound forms of mental activity. If we have a delusion, we are, in effect, a detective on the scent of a case, picking up clues all over the place. We're trying to bring in the malefactor. So it enables us to go through life with an hypothesis. For some, it is unendurable to live without some hypothesis. So jealousy becomes one of the most satisfactory delusional schemes.

You have an hypothesis: She or he is not faithful to me. Then you study it. You listen to the voice. You check out alibis. It sharpens one's senses. Jealousy gives us a ride we would not have without it. People often come into love with their senses drugged by all their bad habits — I mean, one of my fundamental theses is that virtually everything in American life works to deaden our senses. The proliferation of plastics first. So, given the fact that we find ourselves in a state of love with senses dulled, we have to sharpen them up. Very often jealousy hones that point. Taking off on a delusional trip keens our instincts. We can feel more alive than we were before if we don't destroy too much en route. Of course, being on the receiving end of jealousy can be abominable. It mickey-mouses you. You're always saying, "No, honey, honest, honey, no, I didn't turn around, no, I didn't look!"

Then there's a lighter form of jealousy that is fascinating. It's jealousy as a way of keeping in touch. Once in a while I'll come home and Norris will say, "What were you doing at three o'clock today?" Not that she does this often, but once in a while. I'll say, "Nothing. I don't know what you're talking about." But then I'll remember, somewhere around three o'clock, *probably* it was three o'clock, I was crossing the street, and I noticed a truly attractive woman. Maybe I turned around and looked at her. It's as if this little act flew through the firmament and lodged in my beloved's head. And at three o'clock she turned around at home and said to herself, "What's that son of a bitch up to?" In that way, that kind of jealousy can be agreeable, can even give you a little glow, oh, God, that dear woman is sure tuned in to me. You see, so that was OK.

MICHELSON: Do you think being in love sharpens psychic connections?

MAILER: Sharpens certain connections at the expense of others. It isn't that love is blind. Love has intense, laser-like tunnel vision, you know, which probably would be a closer way of describing the nature of how love sees.

MICHELSON: One other question: Great artists take risks in their work. What's the greatest risk you've taken?

MAILER: I tend to do things that are chancy, but I wouldn't necessarily dignify them with the word risk. Maybe my novel about Egypt is the one that's —

MICHELSON: The one you're working on now?

MAILER: Yes — is the one most filled with risk. What do we mean by risk? Do you mean going wrong in a book? In other words, embarking on a book so ambitious that you can fall on your face?

MICHELSON: Yes.

MAILER: Maybe the book on Egypt qualifies for that.

MICHELSON: One final question. What have you told your daughters and sons about sex?

MAILER: One of my daughters was talking once about losing her virginity, and I said, "Oh, God, don't lose it because you come to that decision. Lose it because you can't help yourself. Because you are so attracted to the guy that it happens." That's the sum of my sexual wisdom. Ah, I don't think she took my advice. (*laughter*)

1981

Prisoner of Success

An Interview with Paul Attanasio

❧

PAUL ATTANASIO: I guess the obvious first question would be: Why another Marilyn book?*

NORMAN MAILER: Well, after the reception, I'm asking myself that question. (*laughs*) I did it because I wanted to, and I thought everybody would say, you know, "Hurrah for Norman Mailer, isn't he a virtuoso?" Instead, they said, "That outrageous slanderer!" I was intrigued with trying again. I never was satisfied with the first book, *Marilyn*. I felt that it had an awful lot to say *about* her but that she never necessarily emerged, she was never a presence. So I wanted to try and do her from the inside — see if I could.

I must say Marilyn fascinates me. She's an angelic witch. There are very few witches who arrive at immense celebrity, very few; the nature is to be secretive. And I've always been fascinated with angels, the idea that certain women have something angelic about them. It's a profoundly sentimental idea, in fact, it's so sentimental it goes beyond being sexist: It's probably — could you say, machoist?

ATTANASIO: I agree with you that it is fascinating. I think one of the problems with the Women's Liberation movement, which I think did a tremendous amount of good, mostly for men —

MAILER: I think that's a good point. I think it did more good for men than for women.

---

* *Of Women and Their Elegance.* Simon & Schuster, 1980.

129

ATTANASIO: I think a lot of it was harmful in that it tried to flatten the differences, and make things a whole lot less interesting.

MAILER: I think it succeeded in wrecking the Democratic Party. Ever since the Women's Movement came along, there hasn't been a Democratic politician who's dared to open his mouth and let anything more forceful than oatmeal come out.

ATTANASIO: One thing that struck me about the book, though, was that I didn't think it was progressive in the way almost every other one of your books was. I thought that probably no other writer in America could do it, but I didn't think you were doing things that you hadn't done in previous books.

MAILER: Except for entering a woman's mind. I barely tried that before: maybe Elena's letter in *The Deer Park*. I've always been afraid to try. In *The Executioner's Song* I was able to get into a great many women's minds, but I didn't feel I had *done* it — I felt it had come about, you know, just because they were wonderful subjects for interview. And so I'd say that the nearest I'd come before on my own was April's mind in *The Executioner's Song*. Practically everything she said was in interviews, but I had to put it together.

That was the only thing I felt was new in *Elegance*. I confess I wanted to do one book where I wasn't stretching. It had been a big stretch on *The Executioner's Song*, and my book about Egypt is a huge stretch, so huge that I walk around winded most of the time in relation to it. And I thought, "I want a little vacation." And it may be that the book suffers from that.

ATTANASIO: You dismiss the whole fact/fiction debate. Do you think any of it is useful, or just a lot of wind?

MAILER: I think it's a dumb debate. If a novelist can take someone who's a legendary figure and invent episodes for them that seem believable, then they've done something wonderful. There's that meeting between J. P. Morgan and Henry Ford in *Ragtime* — I think it's one of the best chapters in American literature. It told me an awful lot about Morgan and an awful lot about Henry Ford, and the fact that it obviously never took place made it even more delicious. When you know the kind of bias and warp with which historians write their history — they're dealing with 10,000 facts and they select 300 very careful ones to make their case, and call that stuff history when we all know it's fiction. The mark of a great historian is that he's a great fiction writer. Very few novels are ever true works of the imagination — I mean, how many Kafkas have there been?

I'm not trying to avoid the fact and fiction argument to protect myself. There's one thing that did worry me in the book with Marilyn. I invented an episode for her that was possibly more extreme than anything in her life. And that gave me pause; I'm worried about it, I'm still worried about it, I think I'd feel less bad about it if I'd done it with a man. I start thinking, "Well, my God, what if after I'm dead somebody writes about me and they put me in a homosexual orgy, which I've never been in, I would detest that, wherever I'd be." And I wrote it — this'll sound incredibly demented — but I wrote it with the idea that Marilyn, wherever she is, would accept this treatment of her. But it's a large assumption.

So I do have a continuing uneasiness about that part of the book. On the other hand I do feel that there's no portrait without it.

ATTANASIO: As far as I can tell, no major figure has appeared in American fiction to provide the sort of Oedipal relationship that you've said you had with Hemingway, nobody to beat out and admire at the same time.

MAILER: Well, it could be said that, on the face of it, he had more talent than anyone coming afterwards, which I think is true. I think Hemingway *and* Faulkner were immensely talented men. I've always felt that way about Faulkner — he just stands out. Hemingway I've had my ups and downs. But I must say after *The Executioner's Song* I realized how very talented he was.

It's obvious why Faulkner had that huge influence on Southern writers. I think that the only metaphor that you can use is that Southern writers are on a rockface, and at the very top of the climb there's that dreadful overhang, Mr. Faulkner.

Hemingway's different. Hemingway occupied the center in every way, not only coming from the Midwest, but he occupies the very center of writing itself. Anyone who's ever read a newspaper can feel how good a writer he is — he uses a vocabulary that if anything is smaller than the average newspaperman's vocabulary. And he does wonderful things with it. So no matter how serious or superficial a reader you are you sense very quickly that you are in the hands of someone who truly can write well. Then, of course, he wrote about things that are very, very interesting to men. There aren't very many women going around saying Hemingway is a great writer. I'm willing to bet more American women who are good writers have been influenced by Proust than by Hemingway. But for men he's central: the anxieties he feels about being a man cover all our anxieties; it's almost impossible *not* to identify with his work.

I just think that nobody has come along since who occupies as much terrain as he does. There were stages in my life when I had something remotely resembling his ambition, but that man had it from the time he was twenty to the time he died. I think he finally packed it in because he wasn't going to sit around and be the Shah of Iran of American letters.

ATTANASIO: Tom Wolfe suggested in his introduction to *The New Journalism* that journalism has sort of usurped the novel since the mid-'60s.

MAILER: I think it's self-serving of Wolfe to say that, because he's a journalist. I've said a hundred times that I think journalism is easier than novel writing because you know the story. I mean, give me a good story that history wrote for me, and I'm content — all I've got to do then is write it. The difficulty of writing a truly impressive novel is equal to asking a singer of the stature of Pavarotti to compose his own music. Journalism makes opera singers of novelists. We've got the story, now all we've got to do is go in and show our vocal cords.

ATTANASIO: What about Vietnam? Do you think it's significant that great movies were made out of the war, but not great books?

MAILER: I haven't thought about it before. If a great war novel's to be written again — and it may be that the great war novel is a form that's now past, it could come fifty years after the war in Vietnam as *War and Peace* came after the Napoleonic Wars. Because I don't think that war will finally be comprehended until we have that perspective. The Second World War accelerated America into a direction it was trying to get into anyway — America was trying to move from one form of capitalism into another; and the government was trying to get into the act.

Vietnam, however, either injured America permanently, so that we may never be the most important nation in the world again, or it may have been an incredible crucible in which the national character shifted and changed. That perspective awaits us yet. But when it comes, I think there may be some incredible stuff done about it, and we may have great novels about Vietnam. And they may be great the way *War and Peace* was great, because the Napoleonic Wars changed Russia forever.

ATTANASIO: What do you look for in a novel or short story when you read?

MAILER: Well, I look for something that's probably different from what anyone else would. I'm searching for very special little tools that I can add to my toolbox. After all, I've been a working craftsman for thirty-five years, and any mechanic or carpenter who works that long acquires a great many tools. I'll also read for other things — to stimulate my flagging interest in narrative. For instance, I reread all of Chandler last summer because he's got such narrative drive.

ATTANASIO: I think there's got to be a new aesthetic of fiction now, a new generation of writers. Do you have any idea —

MAILER: What the direction will be? I think we're lumbered right now in fiction. There are many too many ideologies that prevail. The women are pleasing the Women's Movement much too much to ever let loose and really write; the men are trying to strike stances; nobody's free of the aftereffects of psychoanalysis yet — there's no confidence among most young novelists that they know more about human nature than psychiatrists. I just read a little bit of Ann Beattie — it's not fair, because I didn't read that much of her — but on the basis of those two short stories, it did remind me that whenever fiction doesn't know where it's going, then there's a tendency to return to the novel of manners. And for a very good reason: Manners are always changing, and it's fascinating how they change, and we can always tell a great deal about society itself if we study manners.

That's the fallback position. But it's a dead end — it gives pleasure, but it doesn't give knowledge. My idea finally is that fiction is a noble pursuit, that ideally it profoundly changes the ways in which people perceive their experience. You know, one Tolstoy, in my mind, is worth maybe 10,000 very good writers.

ATTANASIO: I have an idea that *The New Yorker* is probably the most pernicious single influence on American fiction writers.

MAILER: Well, it is if one would like to see things bust loose. They were a million miles away from Kerouac and Ginsberg when the Beat Movement started. So they're awful at such periods. But on the other hand, they hold the act together when nothing's happening. They're kind of like those actors of the second category who keep repertory companies going forever, and without them there might not be theater.

ATTANASIO: I wanted to talk a little bit about your personal life —

MAILER: Good luck!

ATTANASIO: It just strikes me that whenever I bring you up, people don't say "Oh, I read *Why Are We in Vietnam?*, it's a great book," they say, "Did you see that thing about the marriages? Mailer's up to his old shenanigans." Something like your marriages is used as a lever against your work.

MAILER: It is. I don't argue with you. Every time I appear in a newspaper I injure myself professionally. But I don't think there's anything I can do about it. One of the reasons I'm in the papers all the time is that they just keep using the same people, over and over again. It's a game, and there are something like forty players on the board. If I were in a Tarot deck, I'd be the Fool. I used to keep a stern separation between the public legend and myself, but you know, you get older, and after a while, you start to feel like some old slob in Miami, with slits in his sneakers so his feet won't hurt so much. At that point it's harder to fight the legend.

ATTANASIO: One thing about your life that was distressing to admirers of yours: during the '60s, whenever there was a march on Washington, your name was mentioned, and now it seems that whenever there's a society article, you're mentioned.

MAILER: I'm a novelist and I want to know every world. And I would never close myself off to a world unless it's truly repulsive to me. I don't think it means anything if I go to certain kinds of parties, because society is nothing if not fashion. There've been a few homes that invite me for dinner from time to time. If it comes to the point where there's something to fight for and I'm not fighting for it because I don't want to lose my position in society, then there's something to be concerned about. But what's there to march for these days? I just can't get excited about stopping those nuclear plants — I think they're the enemy, yes, but I don't think they're the real enemy. I think big oil and plastics are.

Suppose the Reagan Administration gets us to the point where we're marching on the Pentagon again, and at that point I'm not marching because that might lose me my ticket at certain dinner parties — then I've turned. But up to that point, my feeling is: "Hey, man, that's my wad you're talking about."

ATTANASIO: I guess I was just wondering how important a part of your life this sort of thing was.

MAILER: What's very important to me is knowing how the world works. I think what ruins most writers of talent is that they don't get enough experience to learn, so their novels always tend to have a certain paranoid perfection which isn't as good as the rough edge of reality. If *The Executioner's Song* had a big effect on people, it was because it wasn't a paranoid work. It had all the rough edges of reality. If I had conceived that book in my imagination, it would have been much more perfect and much less good.

If there's a theme that obsesses me, it's how much of the history that's made around us is conspiracy and how much of it is simple stupid fuckups. And you have to know the world to get some idea of it. You know, how much does the Mafia control, how much do they luck into? How much does the Jewish community affect the mentality of government, and how much are they accused of?

On the other hand, it's very dangerous to live in society too much, because it's a world of very rigid rules. You cannot be yourself completely. There's a marvelous game in society, which is: If you are completely of society, then you're totally uninteresting. If I have any entree at all it's because society is always fascinated with mavericks. Till the point where they'll become bored with me, and then, boom, I'm out. But on the other hand, even as a maverick there are certain rules that I have to obey. If you start obeying those rules past the point where you want to go along with them as part of the game, then you are injuring yourself.

I don't think it's basic to me. For one thing, I could never cut a figure in society the way, say, Truman did. So I don't really think about it that much. I think if I had had these experiences twenty years ago, I might have saved myself a lot of time as a writer.

ATTANASIO: I know you gave speeches earlier in the year for Kennedy. How do you feel about the Reagan victory? Does it scare you? Maybe not just Reagan himself, but the people who put him in office?

MAILER: I think we're going to have the biggest money-grab since the Grant Administration. Beefing up the defense plants is the health of any major economy, no matter how glutted and wasteful it is. You can't go wrong on a war economy for five or ten years. So I think they're going to go in that direction, because it'll solve every problem they've got.

Then they're going to try to increase states' rights; all those lobbyists won't have to run through the tough work of having to push something through Congress, they'll be able to buy up state legislatures. And then the ecology business is going to be a disaster, because there's an awful lot of money to be made if we can just violate nature a little more. So there could be incredible scandals, and if that happens, and the thing looks like it's in danger of falling apart, then that again is a move toward getting more militaristic. The military covers everything. At that moment the trade unions can't beef, and obviously the threat of bringing in martial law everywhere tends to tone things down.

But if it keeps building that way, and the ghettos don't take it passively, we're going to have a hell of a situation.

ATTANASIO: Do you think there'll be that sense there was in the '50s? I know you've said that in the '50s, there was a sense that there was a war going on, for the writers.

MAILER: I think it'll clean up the left a lot; I think they'll start examining themselves. You know, the left has been guilty of overweening vanity for the last twenty years. First the left was too militant and too programmatic and took itself much too seriously and thought it was creating vast revolutions when in fact it was only creating small middle-class revolutions. Then the Women's Movement came along and — I'll say one good thing about it: The Women's Movement did alert us to the notion that women systematically were being brought up to be cowards, and that was onerous. To this extent the men have learned a lot, and the women have learned . . . something. Less than men have. Because we've changed our view of women; I don't think the women of Women's Liberation have changed their view of men, which isn't worth printing anyway. But you know the women on the left have just been abominable, guilty of infantile leftism of the worst sort, as Lenin defined it.

ATTANASIO: Which is — ?

MAILER: Pushing for one's own demands to the exclusion of all else. Refusing to see the total picture, the total need. A great inner discipline, perhaps, within the enclave, but no interface with other leftist disciplines.

I think now, if the left is threatened from the outside, that might be healthy. The '70s have been a disaster period for the left, which culminated in the Carter Administration. The blandness, the lack of ideas that anyone was even remotely willing to die for. I think the left functions best on adversity. But I think we've got to open our horizons. Marx would've been appalled at the narrowness of his followers.

1980

A Brief Exchange

*with Anita Eichholz**

❧

ANITA EICHHOLZ: You said that the Women's Movement tends to become totalitarian and that you don't like that. Don't you think the male system in America is totalitarian?

NORMAN MAILER: Yes, but I always thought women had more sense than men.

EICHHOLZ: Why is that? Why should women be better than men?

MAILER: Because they have been forced to suffer our brutalities and our stupidities and our dominance and people that are on the bottom should always be smarter than people on top, or there is no hope for humanity.

EICHHOLZ: But you don't get better by suffering.

MAILER: You don't get a better person, but you should get a smarter one. I think that the average black knows more about life than the average white in America. I've never met — this is a remark that I've made before and people think I'm blowing smoke — I've never met a stupid black man. I've met any number of black men I couldn't speak to, who wouldn't talk to me or I couldn't talk to them, but I never met a black who I felt was stupid. Because stupidity is a choice. It's not a choice that black people can afford.

EICHHOLZ: But you can't compare blacks in every respect to women.

---

* This was not an interview but a dialogue in a classroom at the University of Munich.

MAILER: Well, but the women in America do. They say: We are your blacks.

EICHHOLZ: This isn't true in all respects.

MAILER: No, of course not. That's one of the troubles with the Women's Movement. They say a great many things that are not true in all respects but they say it as if it is.

EICHHOLZ: But why can't you answer my question with respect to women? Why should women be smarter than men and do everything better than they and be more clever than they are?

MAILER: There's no reason why they should be better. On the other hand, they should not be worse. Men over the centuries have acquired, willy-nilly, a certain rudimentary sense of fair play. The women have yet to learn it. I think they may. I'm not saying that it is impossible for them. But the Women's Movement over the last ten years has not gained respect among those men who are willing to give it. The general attitude among the women in America by now — I do not pretend to speak for them, it's my impression — is that many mistakes were made ten years ago when the movement first came into prominence, great excesses, and the problem is much more difficult than they ever realized. I think there was a certain optimism, almost a manic optimism, among the women back in the early Seventies. They thought they were going to have a quick breakthrough and change the world very quickly and I think that what they've come to recognize is — and I think this is all to the good — they've come to recognize the profound and serious problems that men who are trying to change the world also have. I think that out of all this we may yet arrive at a certain community of agreement that changing the world is a problem that goes beyond sexual gender.

EICHHOLZ: But you could start with that.

MAILER: You could start with that, but you could start with other notions as well. You could start with the idea that the most evil substance on earth today is plastic and that the way to improve society is to tax plastic heavily and reduce all other taxes. If you could remove plastic from human existence, things might be better because people's senses might be more lively. If people's senses were more lively — for instance, if we were in a room with chandeliers instead of these goddamn fluorescent lights overhead — we might all have a little more communion with one another.

EICHHOLZ: Yes, but that's exactly the problem. The women's question is postponed to all other questions.

MAILER: Well, that's your point of view and I respect it. That the women's question does not have enough prominence. My feeling is that the women have had a huge amount of prominence because the nature of their question was such that television loved it. It made good television — the women having a revolution. But in fact, in America all the women revolutionaries stayed in New York where they were comfortable and safe and very few went down to Texas. It's one thing to be a revolutionary, it's another to be a brave revolutionary. I just say they're not quite as good as they pretend to be.

1980

Waste

An Interview with Michael Lennon

꒛

MICHAEL LENNON: Do you think the election of Reagan might clarify the conflict between right and left?

NORMAN MAILER: Well, I've felt for a long time that liberalism is bankrupt. I think it was trying to do something, let's say from Roosevelt on, that was unique in human affairs. It attempted not only to take care of the top, but to lubricate the bottom. After the Second World War, out of the great guilt many Americans felt at what had been done to black people for two hundred years or more, a decision was made to ameliorate the black condition. A part of the surplus now began to go down to the blacks. Of course, it was still not a tenth of the amount that was being wasted at the top. Nonetheless, America had become the first super-society to attempt, on a major scale, to pay off the top and bottom while allowing the middle to support the ends. Of course, the middle had no cause for complaint. They had chosen the middle precisely because security was there. All the same, the onus of paying was on them. So it created vast resentment, and it was kept focused toward the bottom. Corporate capitalism succeeded, I believe, in convincing Americans that the Democratic Party was supporting people who didn't work, and in a sense, that was true. There were a lot of people in black areas and poor white areas who were ripping off welfare. But they didn't make up a tenth of that patch who were feeding off American society at the top. Just think of the needless expense that goes into products that don't need to be surrounded with romantic appurtenances. You know we don't have to fall in love with our soap. Maybe we do have to love our automobile, but we certainly don't have to admire any number of basic products that have no character to distinguish them. Money that could be put into increasing true competitive quality instead goes into contests with other producers to have zappier advertising. All the while, there has been a tacit agreement between black power and liberal power: "You guys (you blacks) keep the ghettos relatively quiet, and the money will keep coming in." Now the American voter has thrown that out. The resentment they've felt for the last ten years — it's been building all through the '70s — is that blacks are getting away with murder, not working and getting too much. Reagan came in on that wave. He said, in effect, "Let's keep all the waste for ourselves."

When I was running for mayor in '69, a number of people took me aside and said, "Look, welfare is the biggest single problem in New York City. The blacks are ripping it off. Why don't you talk to some of them? If you could ever work out a plan that looks like it makes a little sense, it would be your best chance to show people that you are doing something the other candidates are not doing. Maybe you'll have a chance to get into real contention." So Breslin and I went up to Harlem and met some mothers who represented a welfare organization. One black woman got up to speak: "Mrs. Richbucks over on Park Avenue, she says I'm taking my welfare check and riding around in a Cadillac and you know what I say? I say: 'Fuck her.' My Cadillac is five years old and I have a lot of trouble meeting the payments on it, and she's riding around in a brand-new Cadillac. Mrs. Gold-ass over on Fifth Avenue says, Look at her, she's been married four times and she's got eighteen children and is drawing welfare for each one of them. She's ripping off the government, I say, 'Fuck her.' I may be lying about five of those children but I got the other thirteen to take care of, and I been married three times. Mrs. Gold-ass over on Fifth Avenue, she don't have to get married because she's got lovers all over the place and furs and diamond rings." The black woman finally glared at me and said, "We want our share of the waste," I thought, "Madam, your argument is unanswerable." I came back to headquarters and said, "Fellows, we got no welfare program." Because I knew we weren't going to tell black people, "Please stop taking things you're not entitled to," when they knew the rich were skimming ten times as much. I think this is the key problem the Democratic Party has to face. If they are truly interested in having a country where everybody has something roughly approaching equal opportunity. To get there, we have to re-think every aspect of American politics and American life, but not in the old radical way of "Let's rally the unions." I mean that is crap beyond crap. By now, America is one vast middle-class consumer nation. Here in the '80s we've got to get into absolutely new ways of looking at politics. You could begin a purification process that might flush out American politics. For instance, America at this point is glutted with needless products that depend for their existence on advertising. Pure waste. Wouldn't sell without it. Suppose any product that advertises itself has to pay a tax in proportion to its relative budget for advertising? That might open up opportunities for a good small business to grow by word of mouth. The left, instead of paying lip service to small business, and then opting immediately for every big government solution they can find, might recognize that big government is truly the enemy of the people and the secret and ultimate ally of the corporation. The Democratic left could begin to re-form around the concept that the economy can't have more productivity until it flushes its waste.

LENNON: Reagan's going to increase the glut.

MAILER: Oh, I think he is an open invitation to big business to take more of a grab. It staggers me how corporate capitalism is endlessly greedy, even greedier than they need to be for their own good.

LENNON: All the counterculture of the '60s didn't really make a dent in the corporation?

MAILER: No effective dent. The corporation has become more and more powerful, controls more and more. It lowers the real standard of living. We used to have roads where people could have an interesting trip. Now even the most beautiful landscape is rendered monotonous by a superhighway. We put up buildings that are absolutely faceless, without decoration, without character, with flat roofs. They do not exalt us when we look at them, they depress us. Exaltation is also part of our real standard of living. Then we adulterate our food. The average food, not only in America by now, but because we export this crap, the average food all over the world is becoming more and more tasteless, more tortured.

LENNON: TV.

MAILER: TV adulterates human relations. TV does the same thing to human relations that frozen food does to real food. All of this is the blight of corporate capitalism. Corporate capitalism is an incubus on the world quite equal to Soviet Communism.

LENNON: And you say that big government is the enemy of the people?

MAILER: Government bears a resemblance to cell fission. Of a cancerous sort. When a cancer cell can't solve a problem, it divides. That's why they proliferate more quickly than normal cells — they're not equipped to solve problems, only to grow. When in doubt, divide; that's cancer. Government proliferates all the time. It doesn't solve problems.

LENNON: What would you like to hear somebody say on American television that's new?

MAILER: Just once let somebody say we don't have to stand up to the Russians. Let them come here and die of indigestion. Let the Russians attempt to take over America. They will perish. Americans would love the idea of joining an underground. The greatest blow for liberty that's ever been struck would indeed be rung. The Russians would founder on the shores of America. That idea is never discussed in America. Let me suggest the real force of it by showing the opposite. What if the Russians invited us to occupy them? It would exhaust us as a nation.

LENNON: What did you think of John Anderson?

MAILER: I thought he was boring. A third party candidate should be interesting, because he has no responsibility.

LENNON: Do you think there is a chance for a third major party in the United States?

MAILER: I think Anderson created some ground for the possibility. He showed that people were interested in a third party in America, he did show that. To such extent we may honor his name someday. But I thought he was awfully boring.

LENNON: Do you think a lot of people didn't vote for John Anderson because they thought he didn't have a chance?

MAILER: That's always true of a third party candidate. You lose half your vote in the last week. As election day gets nearer, people want their vote to count. There is a fetishism to voting. One wants to be buried in the proper cemetery. So, if you're a third party candidate, you should be interesting. You have no responsibilities, you don't have to worry about losing millions of votes for the wrong remark; you're going to lose them anyway. But Anderson had nothing new to offer. He didn't understand that his simple duty was to be interesting.

1980

The Mad Butler

An Interview with Hilary Mills

ֆ

HILARY MILLS: Looking back on your career, it seems as if your novel *The Deer Park* was a kind of watershed. It was after that book came out in 1955 that you gradually moved away from the novel and into journalism. What happened at that point in your career?

NORMAN MAILER: I think the watershed book was *Advertisements for Myself.* That was the first to be written in what became my style. I never felt as if I had one until that book, and once I developed the style — for better or for worse — a lot of other forms opened to it.

MILLS: You've mentioned previously that you were smoking a lot of marijuana around this time; do you think this had anything to do with the difficulties you were encountering in your work?

MAILER: No. All it did was consume large tracts of my brain. I was doing to my brain what Barry Goldwater recommended we do to the foliage in Vietnam. I think parts of my head have been permanently sluggish ever since. But I don't think the damage to my head was what was giving me difficulty in writing. It was more timidity. I was a little aghast at what I was trying to do because no one had ever done it before. These days everybody is laying claim to having started the New Journalism. Tom Wolfe has been writing manifestos for the last ten years. But I think if I started any aspect of the New Journalism — and I did — it was an enormously personalized journalism where the character of the narra-

145

tor was one of the elements not only in telling the story but in the way the reader would assess the experience.

I had some dim instinctive feeling that what was wrong with all journalism was that the reporter pretended to be objective and that was one of the great lies of all time. What this really was, was an all-out assault on *New Yorker* writing, and at the same time I had — as all of us did — a vast respect for *The New Yorker*. So I was a little scared at what I was doing. I thought I was either all right or all wrong. The stakes were high, but by now it's more comfortable to write that way.

MILLS: You also pointed out in *Cannibals and Christians* that after the war American society was changing so rapidly that "the novel gave up any desire to be a creation equal to the phenomenon of the country." Did this have anything to do with your move away from the novel form and into journalism?

MAILER: Well, I wasn't taking journalism that seriously.

The thing that makes the novel so hellishly difficult is that you have to elucidate a story from the material. If you make a mistake then you may not discover it until the book is done and you're looking back on it ten years later. It's very much like chess in a funny way. Good chess players always speak of the best line of continuation. They can analyze a game afterward and replay the points of no return and see whether a knight should have been moved to another square. In the novel, you're left wondering.

MILLS: You've talked a lot about your economic problems in the past. If economic necessity hadn't been a factor in your life, would you have written as much as you have?

MAILER: No. I would have written books that are more literary and more well-rubbed, and I would have spent more time on them.

MILLS: Would all these books have been novels or would you have written journalism anyway?

MAILER: I could have gotten into journalism, particularly with the history we had in the Sixties. I'd never come up with a story of my own that was as good as the things that were happening all through the Sixties.

MILLS: So in a sense there has never been a conscious or premeditated orchestration of your own career; it just happened the way it did?

MAILER: Yes. I've always been reacting to the given.

MILLS: There seems to be a kind of tragic irony in American literary life: The youngest writers with the most brilliant first novels are the ones subjected to the most horrendous pressures. How would you say your early success affected you and your work?

MAILER: It changed my life. For a long time after the success of *The Naked and the Dead,* for seven or eight years, I kept walking around saying nobody treats me as if I'm real, nobody wants me for myself, for my five-feet eight-inches, everybody wants me for my celebrity. Therefore my experience wasn't real. All the habits I'd formed up to that point of being an observer on the sidelines were shattered. Suddenly, if I went into a room I was the center of the room, and so regardless of how I carried myself, everything I did was taken seriously and critically. I complained bitterly to myself about the unfairness of it until the day I realized that it was fair, that that was my experience. It's the simplest remark to make to yourself, but it took me ten years to get to that point.

Then I began to realize the kind of writing I was going to do would be altogether different from the kind of writing I thought I would do. After *The Naked and the Dead* I wanted to write huge collective novels about American life, but I knew I had to go out and get experience and my celebrity made it impossible. I then began to realize that there was something else that I was going to get which hopefully would be equally valuable, and that was that I was having a form of twentieth-century experience which would become more and more prevalent: I was utterly separated from my roots. I was successful and alienated and that was a twentieth-century condition. This went into all my work after that in one way or another and will go on forever because by now I suppose I can say that kind of personality interests me more than someone who is rooted.

MILLS: Do you ever think of an audience when you write?

MAILER: No. I used to have a much clearer idea of who I was writing for — certain friends, certain intellectuals, certain critics, a clearer sense of the kind of audience I wanted out there and who they might be. That was in the Sixties, but in the Seventies there was a stretch where I really didn't know who I was writing for. You go in and out of fashion and your sense of who you're writing for goes in and out of focus. I must say with my Egyptian book I've gotten to the point where I don't care. I wouldn't have a clue who's going to like it. You get old enough and realize there are no literary gods left. That's not bad; there's something demeaning about being in awe of a critic.

MILLS: Is your concentration different when you work on a novel from when you work on journalism?

MAILER: The novel is much more demanding physically. I've found that I can't do serious writing without getting into a depression. The depression is a vital part of the process because, to begin with, it's dangerous beyond measure to fall in love with what you're doing while you're doing it. You lose your judgment and you lose it for the simplest reason — that the words, as you're reading them, are stirring you too much. The odds are, if they're stirring you too much, they are going to stir no one else.

MILLS: Are you one of those writers who build a book painstakingly from page one or do you like to get the material down and go back and revise?

MAILER: I'm not happy if I feel that what's behind me is wrong or needs work. I tend to build my books on the basis of what I have already. I never have a master plan for the entire book. Every time I have — and when I was younger I used to sit down and write out a complete plan for a book — I never wrote the book. Even with *The Executioner's Song* where, after all, I knew the story in great detail, I was very careful not to be versed in too many details of the story way ahead. In other words, I tended to do my research let's say 100 pages ahead of where I was because I wanted to keep the feeling that I didn't know how it was all going to turn out. I wanted to have the illusion that I was inventing each little detail as if I were writing a conventional novel.

MILLS: Do you ever show your manuscript pages to someone while a work is in progress?

MAILER: Oh sure. I do it the way I box: I pick my sparring partners carefully. Usually I'll box with people who are so good that I'm in no danger of being hurt because they consider it obscene to damage me. Or I'll box with friends where we understand each other and are trying to bring out the best in each other as boxers. The same thing with an early stage of a manuscript. I'd no more dream of showing it to someone like John Simon than I would of carrying a kite to the Brooklyn Bridge and jumping off. But I'll show it to Norris or to Bob Lucid, who is a great friend of mine, or to Scott Meredith, my agent.

MILLS: You've worked on a number of other books while writing your big novel. Do you ever find it hard to get back in sync with the novel after doing these other projects?

MAILER: I've often said that this Egyptian novel is nicer to me than any of my wives. I leave it for two years and come back and it says, "Oh you look tired, you've been away, here let me wash your feet." I've been able to go back to it without trouble every time so far. But a novel is very much like that mythological creature: a good woman. You can't abuse her forever. So I think I've finally got to finish the Egyptian novel. The time has come.

MILLS: What is it about?

MAILER: It takes place in the reign of Ramses IX who was pharaoh in the twentieth dynasty. The period is 1130 B.C. That's just the first novel. I'm two-thirds of the way through, and it's 1,000 pages long so far. The second novel will take place in the future and a third novel will be contemporary. I've got a tricky way of tying them up, but I'm not going to talk about that.

MILLS: Can you just say what the original inspiration for the book was?

MAILER: I thought I'd take a quick trip through Egypt. At one point I wanted the novel to be picaresque and have a chapter on Egypt of antiquity, a chapter on Greece, and a chapter on Rome just to show how marvelously talented I was to be able to do all these things. So I dipped into Egypt and never got out. I'm kind of sluggish when you get right down to it.

MILLS: Your work is totally unique, but do you see yourself as a direct descendent of any particular literary line?

MAILER: My taste and my loyalties are all in separate places. My loyalties are to people like Dreiser and Farrell and maybe Steinbeck and Wolfe — all the people who were writing about working-class and lower middle-class people. They were the ones who first got me excited about writing. On the other hand, my taste quickly inclined toward Hemingway and Faulkner and Fitzgerald and I learned many things from them that I didn't from the other bunch. Then, in a way, my actual influences are so peculiar. Henry Adams, for instance, obviously had a vast influence on me but I never knew he did until I started to write *The Armies of the Night.*

MILLS: Are you in the habit of socializing a lot with other writers?

MAILER: I think the literary world is a dangerous place to be in if you want to do an awful lot of writing because it's almost necessary to take on airs in order to protect yourself in that world. In a way you can't handle yourself skillfully unless your airs are finely tuned. Capote has a wonderful set and walks around like a little fortress — at least until lately. There are starting to be some cracks in the wall.

Hemingway committed suicide working on those airs. He took

the literary world much too seriously and he's almost there as a lesson to the rest of us: Don't get involved in that world at too deep a level or it will kill you and kill you for the silliest reasons: for vanity and because feuds are beginning to etch your liver with the acids of frustration.

MILLS: On the other hand, you've put almost as much creative energy into your public performing self as you have into your work. Do you think that public self has helped or hurt your work?

MAILER: It's probably helped my mind and hurt my work. I think I've had the kind of experience that made me equipped to deal with certain kinds of problems that a writer who's more serious about keeping to his study and not venturing out too much — or certainly not venturing out on quixotic ventures — would not have had. I think I have an understanding of the complexity of the world that I wouldn't have if I'd stayed at home. I would have tended to have a much more paranoid vision of how sinister things are. Things are sinister but not in the way I used to think.

MILLS: It's interesting that in your latest books, *The Executioner's Song* and *Of Women and Their Elegance,* Norman Mailer is conspicuously absent as narrator. Is this a conscious attempt on your part to get away from the autobiographical mode?

MAILER: I think I've worn out my feeling that that was the style in which to keep writing. It was so difficult for me to arrive at my own style — I didn't start with an identity. I forged an identity through my experience. Because of that, I think it was easier to give up that style when the time came. I didn't feel as if I were giving myself away.

And then I've always felt as if the way people react to me is not to me but to the latest photograph they've seen of me. So I can change the photograph and have the fun of observing the reactions. The devil in me loves the idea of being just that much of a changeling. You can never understand a writer until you find his private little vanity and mine has always been that I will frustrate expectations. People think they've found a way of dismissing me, but, like the mad butler — I'll be back serving the meal.

1980

An Author's Identity

An Interview with Michael Lennon

⚘

MICHAEL LENNON: To what do you attribute your ability to move from style to style?

NORMAN MAILER: Some writers have a powerful sense of identity. I think the best American example might be Henry Miller. Hemingway too. Faulkner, Thomas Wolfe. Then you get to people like Steinbeck who kept changing his identity with every book he did. I could add myself or Ed Doctorow as other good examples of this second category. I suppose our personality becomes an index to us of how the world is changing. So the act of writing serves us differently than it does Hemingway or Miller. For them, writing works as an assertion of their existence.

LENNON: Picasso went through many styles and it's been attributed by some to his various marriages. Is that true in your case to any extent? Have your relations with your families had a major impact in some underground fashion?

MAILER: Picasso did work in a new vein for every wife. I could say the same about myself up to a point. I suppose I've written a different book with every wife but then I think you become a different man in each marriage. On the other hand, Miller was married many times and that did not change his identity.

LENNON: So what is the crucial difference between you and Miller?

MAILER: Some people are born with clear roots. They know exactly where they came from and who they are and what they are, but the world is mysterious to them. I've always been the opposite —

151

sensitive to the world and forever in the course of discovering who I am and what I am.

LENNON: Well, I was also going to say you and Miller are both from Brooklyn and Miller has written some about his early life there. You've said your childhood never interested you very much. You didn't really want to write about it. Could it be that you had no sense of reacting against your childhood the way Miller reacted against his German bourgeois roots? What did he say, "My family were Nordic, which is to say idiots." Of course, you had close ties with your family. You still live there. But you never were reacting for or against Brooklyn. Maybe you were freer to move than Miller, in a sense?

MAILER: Well, I was close to my parents. I didn't have to break away. I never had a sense of fighting my way clear. In fact, the outside world was much tougher. Maybe the difference is right there. Someone like Miller had to establish his identity very early in life. If he didn't, a large part of him would have been ruined for any kind of serious effort later in life. I expect this is true for people who grow up in hostile families — they must establish their identities early. So there is often a rock-hard quality to the personality. Hemingway may have had subtler problems in his family, but he also had to establish his identity. Whereas my mother and my father treated my sister and myself as important people. At home, we were the center of their universe. It was the outside world that was difficult. So I was always terribly alert to the street and took the family hearth for granted. I was free to indulge myself there.

LENNON: You've said that some of your best writing comes out of your worst periods and that you sometimes have to go through the bends to accomplish what you want.

MAILER: I'm a little uneasy when writing doesn't come hard. It's better for me when I have to forge the will to do it on a given day. I find looking back, and I can't even tell you why, that on the days it was very hard, but I finally did succeed, and the same occurred next day and the next and the next, each day writing against great resistance in myself and finishing in great depression, that those became the best things I did. *The Armies of the Night* was written in a towering depression. I did it in two months and those were some of the worst weeks in my life. I would come home each night and think it was terrible.

LENNON: You said that when you were attempting to get started on

Armies, you finally tried the third person and it worked for you. Was that a release of some pressure?

MAILER: No, it merely shifted the pressure. On the one hand, it seemed interesting to speak of a protagonist named Norman Mailer, on the other it was odd. I remained uncomfortable with it for quite a period. I'd say I was halfway into the book before I got used to it. It took me longer than any reader. You may remember how the style felt when you started reading the book.

LENNON: It was a shock.

MAILER: It's a very funny way to look at oneself.

LENNON: Nevertheless, it was like an old shoe by the time you got rid of it.

MAILER: Yes, by the time I was done, I missed it so much I kept going back in book after book. It never worked as well again.

LENNON: I think you said in *The Fight* that you were getting tired of that style. Is that correct?

MAILER: I got less and less interested in myself. In *The Armies of the Night* I was a true protagonist of the best sort, which is half-heroic and three-quarters comic. That makes for a marvelous protagonist.

LENNON: Like a Stendhal hero?

MAILER: No, no. Nothing like. Nothing so large.

LENNON: No, but still, you had a success and you had a failure, you were on top of it, you were sick of yourself. That's a little bit like Julien Sorel, I think.

MAILER: Except he had this vast project. He was going to become one of the mightiest men in France. All I wanted to do, if you remember, was get to a dinner party that night.

LENNON: I always think of *The Armies of the Night* as a nineteenth-century novel.

MAILER: There is no sex. In that sense, it's a nineteenth-century novel. It's courtly, it's deliberate, it's amused with its time and place. It's taken for granted that its characters are all very fine and substantial people. We know it's going to turn out well in the end. I suppose it has the restrained merriment of the early nineteenth-century picaresque novel. I guess I have to agree.

LENNON: Do you think that you can influence society in some way by writing? Or change society?

MAILER: When I was young, I used to believe you could do it with one book, apocalyptically. Now I know one has very little effect. You can't even measure the results of your books.

LENNON: Do you worry about bruising the readers' sensibilities ever?

MAILER: Anyone who worries about whether they are going to hurt somebody's feelings by their work is no more a writer than a surgeon who would say to himself, "In making this incision I'm going to give this young woman a scar on her belly that could injure her love life for the next thirty years." The surgeon says, "Scalpel, nurse," and makes the cut. He may be right or wrong in the need for the operation, but he keeps a certain insensitivity to other parts of the context. Writers also have to have their own kind of blindness. They can't say to themselves, "This portrait of my good friend is going to scar him terribly." If they feel that, they can't write. Indeed, a great many young writers can't. They think of all the people they're going to hurt, or those they're going to make enemies of, and the retribution that will come, and it doesn't seem worth it to them. There has to be something a bit maniacal about a young man or woman who wants to write. He has to be willing to get that book out no matter how many psychic corpses are left en route, or who is coming after him later.

LENNON: But what sort of responsibility do you have?

MAILER: Never to take the immediate advantage. Never to cash those easy checks. It's very dangerous when you are writing to milk it, to say to oneself, I have a prize cow and the price of milk is high now. I'm going to get every last bit of milk out. You have to be very careful of that. Writing may be an instinctive process, but it's not always clear. You often feel no more than a dull pressure from your instinct to go here or go there. You have to try to listen to the faint voice that tells you how to stay true to the work. Very hard to do. A writer's open to every pressure to take the immediate advantage, whatever it is. We all do in various ways.

LENNON: I think Faulkner said at one point, "A good book is worth a thousand old grandmothers, a thousand old women. And if it were necessary to get rid of the old grandmothers to write a good book, then it would be well worth it." Do you agree with that?

MAILER: No, a thousand is too many. Three or four, maybe.

LENNON: Do you believe that a movie has more possibilities to influence modern people than literature?

MAILER: I think good movies are more likely to reach deep feelings in people.

LENNON: Why? Because it's visual?

MAILER: Because movies are more primitive, I would argue, than literature. Film directs itself to more primitive states of consciousness. People who can't read get profound reactions out of movies. I would also say that to the degree that film reaches us in a precise way, it's no good. Film is best when ambiguous. A truly good film will affect two people profoundly, but they'll argue for hours over the message. One might say it is a satire, the other, a tragedy. That's as it should be. Film should reach way inside the psyche and prove truly disturbing. One person can go through horror watching a film, another person laugh their head off. That's good film. Bad film is when everybody laughs on cue. Then they are being manipulated. They have merely entered the engines of manipulation of the great institutions.

LENNON: You talk a lot about manipulation. Is there anything in life that is not in some sense manipulation?

MAILER: Yes. An existential situation.

LENNON: Doesn't everybody manipulate somebody else?

MAILER: If I'm manipulating you and you're manipulating me, that's interesting. That has elements of the game in it. One of us wins, the other loses. But at least we're both doing it on relatively fair terms. When you have huge institutions manipulating us, it isn't fair. Fair play, that's all I ask for.

LENNON: Well, you call yourself an existentialist. You speak of returning to the instinctual self. Yet you take notice of habit, discipline, even pretense and compromise as sort of civilized qualities that are more or less necessary. I'd like to know how one can be an existentialist in the modern world.

MAILER: You're asking me a small question. (*laughter*) To begin with, habit and discipline are absolutely necessary to serious projects. That doesn't mean we can ignore the fact that the habits which enable us to be productive are dangerous to our psyche. They keep us from living existentially. Now, when I say existentially, I don't mean that every day we must jump from the roof of one building to the roof of another. Although this is certainly as existential an experience as one could look for. Especially if the jump is at the very limit of our ability to leap. If we do not know whether we're going to be able to make the jump successfully, that would be a pure existential experience. We're going to feel a great rush of adrenaline and happiness if we complete the leap, or know disaster and death if we don't. Obviously, if I speak of living counter to one's habits, I don't mean jumping across the roof every day. However, it may be that one has to leap across that figurative roof once a month, or once a year, or whatever one's inner rhythm is. If one uses discipline to accomplish serious projects in one's life, there comes a point where one becomes a slave of the habit, and one must look then for an existential encounter. But the idea is not that we all go out and climb the Matterhorn every Saturday. It may be that someone who is timid and gentle and reflective and would much rather spend his or her life reading books can still have an existential life. They need only think seriously of climbing the Matterhorn once, or trying it once, and that's enough. For some people, one existential experience is enough nourishment for ten, twenty, thirty years. Other people, like U.S. Marines, need existential experience three times a night. I'm not a bigot about these matters. I don't insist that everybody live the same way.

LENNON: Who would you today consider to be major American authors from your personal perspective? And why?

MAILER: There are probably twenty American authors who if you asked "Who are the major American authors?" would name one writer first — themselves. John Updike would say John Updike, Bellow would say Bellow.

LENNON: What would Norman Mailer say?

MAILER: Norman Mailer, you may depend upon it, would say Norman Mailer. We have a funny situation at present in American letters. There are no giants around. Once we had Hemingway and Faulkner. Now, we're all like spokes in a wheel. You cannot ask, "Who is the major spoke?" Each spoke will reply, "So far as I can feel it, I am the only one."

LENNON: But who, besides yourself?

MAILER: There are a lot of writers for whom I have regard. I think Saul Bellow is a very good writer. John Updike is very good, John Cheever . . .

LENNON: What about Gore Vidal?

MAILER: Vidal is a wit and a good essayist. Not a good novelist.

LENNON: What about Truman Capote?

MAILER: Capote is a stylist and a very good writer, but he's not done anything memorable lately. Of course, he's been working for years on *Answered Prayers*. We'll have to wait and see.

LENNON: Any authors who are overrated?

MAILER: It's hard for an overrated writer to last. There are many more literary critics in America than men or women who can make a living writing novels. We've all been examined and re-examined for twenty or thirty years. So it would be hard for someone *ersatz* to get through.

LENNON: What about Pynchon?

MAILER: Either a genius or vastly overrated. I've never been able to read him. Just can't get through the bananas in *Gravity's Rainbow*.

LENNON: Are there any Latin American writers you are familiar with?

MAILER: Well, I think Borges and Márquez are the two most important writers in the world today.

LENNON: Why Borges? In political terms he is a reactionary, is he not?

MAILER: Well, he is a conservative, but . . . I detest having to think of a writer by his politics first. It's like thinking of people by way of their anus. Borges has this magical ability to take plots and turn them inside out. I sometimes think Borges may do in five pages what Pynchon does in five hundred. Which is, he shows us the resources of the novel. He's a magician's magician. In that sense, I love his work.

LENNON: Márquez?

MAILER: Márquez is wonderful. In *One Hundred Years of Solitude* he created not one world but a hundred. I don't know how Márquez does it. People come into his books. . . . In ten pages he'll create a family that has eighteen children and they go through ten years, and you know every one of the children, and all the events that occur in their life. In ten pages, I have all I can do to get around one bend in the Nile.

1980

Writers and Boxers

An Interview with Michael Lennon

❧

MICHAEL LENNON: Writers, I've heard you say, are a little bit like athletes. And then you said, you never question your instincts. I question your premise. Aren't athletes really very disciplined people?

NORMAN MAILER: Well, I make remarks off the top of my head that have a kernel of truth. Then I have to think about it afterwards. I believe what I actually said was that when it comes to decide which book I'm going to write next, I generally follow my instincts. But not in everything. Why, if I did, I would end up in jail. I think athletes go through their own particular drama. They tend to trust their instincts for a long time — at least the instincts of their body. When they can't, in other words when they follow their deepest instincts and lose their game, they're in more trouble than us. I think athletes first come into contact with despair when their instincts fail them. So with all these amendments, I'll still support the remark.

LENNON: I'm assuming again that instincts are connected to the unconscious in some way. Why can't the unconscious be as error prone as the conscious?

MAILER: You know the famous story of Shelley? He rushed up to a mother, seized a two-month-old infant out of her arms, held up the infant and said, "Babe, speak. Reveal your immortal truth!" He believed the infant was born knowing everything. Like Plato — he was a great Platonist at that point, was Shelley — he believed that the education you receive when you're young obfuscates the instinctive knowledge with which you're born. Then you spend the rest of your life trying to unmake that education. I also believe we're born with a profound appreciation of the universe and lose it in the first few years of our life, then spend the rest of our time trying to gain it back. By the age of six, the school system makes certain we lose it. I don't think this is so evil. It is rather in the nature of things. It was intended that way. We're supposed to lose it and regain it. I think it is impossible to conceive of any real achievement in knowledge without that fall. Because if knowledge is something we receive merely by opening ourselves to it, well — in the West, we can't conceive of that. Most of us find something repellent about Hindu philosophy. It's the idea that you receive wisdom without a Faustian effort. The more you give yourself to the universe, more passive you become, the closer you will be to the secrets of existence. This is profoundly repellent to the Western mind. We feel you get to the kernel of real secrets by smashing the shell. That's the way we want it. It's what we're built to do.

LENNON: Like Melville peeling away the layers of the onion to reach the inmost center?

MAILER: Well, if you're going to peel the layers of the onion, I think we even secretly believe it helps if you cut off a finger or two while peeling. But you say why do *I* trust *my* instincts? Because like a young professional athlete, I never had to think about earning a living until the last ten or fifteen years. From the time I was twenty-five, I knew I was probably going to have enough money to be a writer the rest of my life, and so I could form a habit of consulting my instincts. Most people don't have the leisure to do that. When you have a nine-to-five job, you can't do much with your instincts because your work is a continuation of the very education that buried the instincts in the first place. Which is another reason why young professional athletes are so different.

LENNON: If you had the advantage as a young man of money coming in, at the same time you had some struggles with shifts in your fame and reputation, didn't you? You were twenty-five and . . .

MAILER: I went through the bends. I find an analogy between my own experience and certain boxers. Occasionally you find a prizefighter like Leon Spinks, who becomes champ before he knows whether he can really fight or not. That's terrifying. It happened to me with *The Naked and the Dead.* I can understand

what Spinks went through afterward. I mean all that idiotic behavior after he beat Ali and won the championship came from the
fact that he wasn't ready for it at all. He didn't know whether he
was just a main-event fighter in a small club, or champion of the
world. So he lost all sense of who he was. If you don't have an
identity, it's very important to have established elements you can
refer to. It's not enough to say to yourself, "I'm Heavyweight
Champion of the world," it helps more if you can also say, "Yes,
and I beat Joe Frazier, George Foreman and twenty-two other
tough guys." Spinks could only say, "I beat Muhammad Ali, I
don't know if that's because I am very good, or he is very old." It
has to create a double sense of identity. Every time you have a
thought about yourself, you have to refer to two separate identities: the Champ and the Fraud. Your psychic economy begins to
work twice as hard.

LENNON: After having so much success with *The Naked and the
Dead* you felt you were a false champion?

MAILER: Well, I felt two ways at once. On the one hand, I believed
my reviews, on the other I knew *The Naked and the Dead* had
been influenced by a great many writers who were better than
me. By Hemingway, Farrell, Steinbeck, by Tolstoy, by Thomas
Wolfe, by Dreiser, very much by Dos Passos. In a certain sense it
was not my own book. These literary influences had flowed
through me. I also had to digest the experience of being at war. I
hadn't been a very good soldier. If you took a company, in my
case a short-handed cavalry troop of one hundred men, maybe
seventy-five or eighty soldiers could put up a tent better than me.
So I was a bit of an impostor. On the other hand, I had all these
wonderful reviews. There were times when you could think it
was the greatest book written since *War and Peace.* Given all
that, I had to carry two views of myself. Same with Spinks. He
needed two halves of his mind to receive every compliment. One
half said, "You're wonderful," and the other was always telling
him: "These people are lying to you." That's the nature of obsession. We feel two ways about one question. So obsessions tend
to paralyze, or flake you out.

LENNON: You've compared yourself to Spinks. I've also heard you
call yourself in an interview the Ezzard Charles of Literature. I
thought you were being enormously modest.

MAILER: No, I'd still say that. Compare the true stature of Hemingway and Faulkner to writers like Bellow and Cheever and Updike
and myself, name eight or ten writers who might be the best

writer in America now, John Barth, Bernard Malamud, Pynchon, Algren, go through the list. Name after name. Out of twenty people, none begin to have, myself included, the stature of Hemingway and Faulkner. In that sense, I'd say to anyone who says I'm the most important writer in America today, well, if I am, I'm still the Ezzard Charles of the heavyweight division.

LENNON: You don't think Hemingway's reputation has slipped in the last ten years? People begin to take a close look at his writing and yours and Pynchon and Bellow? You, Pynchon and Bellow are the three I hear.

MAILER: Well, I don't know. We're all vastly more complex in our preoccupations than Hemingway. But I have to tell you that after I wrote *The Executioner's Song*, I went back and looked at Hemingway again. Cause now I was writing in a simple style. And his style *is* remarkable. The more I know about writing, the more of an achievement Hemingway's style becomes to me. I know his flaws inside out. I've loved and hated him as if he were my own father for years. There is so much he did for one, so much he didn't do. Truly the relationship you have to him is as a father. But he is a remarkable writer. His sense of the English language, I'd say, is virtually primitive in its power to evoke mood and stir the senses.

LENNON: What do you think he would think of *Executioner's Song*?

MAILER: He'd hate it and say, "That is bad Hemingway!" He'd loathe the book. But you know, he was a prick, let's face it.

LENNON: Who would you compare Ali to as a writer?

MAILER: Ali is very much like Hemingway if you're going to look for a parallel. First of all, he dominated his division entirely. Second of all, Hemingway, like Ali, put in a considerable apprenticeship. He just didn't become famous, he spent a number of years writing short stories and working on newspapers. He had not had a tremendous amount of experience before he became prominent, but it was more than people realize. Ali also had a number of tough fights before he beat Liston. Then, like Hemingway, he remained champion for a long, long time and kept dominating his division. Very much like Hemingway, very vain in the way Hemingway was vain. Couldn't bear competition, nor the idea that anyone around him might be remotely as good as he is. I think there is a wonderful study to be made about the similarities between Ernest Hemingway and Muhammad Ali. They come out of that same American urgency to be the only planet in existence.

To be the sun. It goes right back to Egypt. A thousand gods but only one sun.

LENNON: Ali's later career isn't quite as brilliant as his early career. Isn't the same thing true of Hemingway?

MAILER: Roughly true. But Ali still did something Hemingway never quite did. After Ali got old, he still won a couple of great fights. He beat Foreman when he was already over the hill. Foreman was an awesome fighter at the point they met. It's one of the great fights of all time because the weaker man won through vast skill and guile and artistry. Plus a dazzling display of guts.

LENNON: Hemingway, at the end, didn't make the big knockout, to use that metaphor, in his later books.

MAILER: No, he did not.

LENNON: I think you once said that one of the best things Hemingway wrote in his later career was the *Paris Review* interview.

MAILER: Yes, that was the best. That, and *A Moveable Feast.*

LENNON: I'd like to go back to *The Naked and the Dead.* I don't think anyone can deny the brilliance of Hemingway in terms of style. But Hemingway could never write a book like *The Naked and the Dead* in which you're talking about fascism coming to America, technology, and the kinds of themes you have dealt with over the past thirty years.

MAILER: I didn't say Hemingway was brighter than I was. I just said he writes better.

LENNON: But that's not the same as saying his talent is better.

MAILER: Well, I think it is. You can have marvelous character actors like Charles Laughton who could play just about any part. Then you get someone like Marilyn Monroe who, in the technical sense, has a small talent. But she can come out and hold a mandolin in her hand and play a little ditty and wonderful things happen. Let's take an example we would argue about less. In the technical sense, there were limitations, I suppose, to Charlie Chaplin. Any number of actors can do a credible imitation of Charlie Chaplin, and, in addition, play fifty roles Chaplin would never go near. Yet we could never argue that they were greater than Chaplin. Even though they might achieve ninety-five percent of him in an imitation, Chaplin plucked a nerve in us that very few artists reach. What great artists do is so profound, you don't debate with it. Ditto, great athletes.

1980

Literary Ambitions

An Interview with Michael Lennon

❧

MICHAEL LENNON: Norman, once or twice when you were asked which of your books you liked the most, you said, "Oh, I don't know. They're like my children. One day I like one more than the other." Yet this analogy breaks down if you believe that a writer must excel in the art of becoming. Don't you see your books as indices of your growth? Or, do you really agree with E. M. Forster that a writer's works are totally distinct tasks, separate from each other? Like children?

NORMAN MAILER: The advantage of being my age is that you can end up agreeing with everyone. What Forster said is true. On the other hand, I go along with you. It's nice if your books can be looked at as indices of growth. I'm just not certain my work has developed that way. I know a great many people would say that *The Executioner's Song* is my best book. And maybe I'd even agree with them. That doesn't mean it shows the most growth. It might present the most digestion. Maybe, I had assimilated my craft at that point, but I wouldn't take it necessarily as a great indication of growth.

LENNON: The best books of George Orwell were usually about things he despised. Are you like Orwell in this respect?

MAILER: I'm drawn to writing about subjects that I feel comfortable with on the one hand and very uncertain of, on the other. For instance, with *The Executioner's Song*, I felt I understood Gilmore's desire to be executed. It seemed to me that if I were in such a situation, I would also want that. It's very real to me that your soul can die before your body. So I felt I can write about this man in a way other people can't. On the other hand, I knew very little about prison, knew nothing about Utah and absolutely nothing about the particular circumstances of Gilmore's life. That was a good balance for me. Let me put it an altogether different way. Years ago, I was considerably taken with how you never know the sure meaning of a Latin sentence until you hear the last syllable of the last word. In Latin if you want to say, "I drink poison from the glass," you can put it in any order you wish. For example: "Poison from the glass drink I." Then the listener wouldn't know who took poison until "drink I" is spoken. That means people had to be alert. It was very easy to trick your neighbor. Now the Romans were the first nation to live consistently in terms of world conquest, and perhaps there was a certain unconscious conspiracy to construct the language that way. So that only the people who were most alert, most unscrupulous, most tricky, and most concerned with getting their way would be adept in the tongue. It was, goes my hypothesis, a language for people seeking power and ready to use all means to obtain it. With that as a key, assuming my key is correct, Latin might become a more fascinating study. Whereas, to approach Latin cold, without a key, would fill me with dismay. In any novel I might write, I like that same possibility present — that I know something other people don't. Those are the books I'm drawn to write. I'm never attracted to a topic where I have no more to say than anyone else.

LENNON: It's become a commonplace to note that your nonfiction is written novelistically. Why?

MAILER: It's nice to end with a book that reads like a novel rather than the digested contents of the first stomach of the cow. Which latter is what most nonfiction is to me. Someone spends a lot of time studying a body of material, they digest it, and write books. They skip the confusions. That's not interesting. We never know the living origins of the conclusions. What is fascinating to me in another writer is how his mind works. If I obtain clues that way, I can improve my own mind. But to suppose an author can digest a subject so well that there is no need to think about the subject independently is disagreeable. So I don't like the way most nonfiction is done. Whereas the novel changes our lives to some extent. Marriages have broken up, for instance, because someone read a novel and decided the life of the character in the book was more interesting than their own. Good novels are painful to read. That's why few people do.

LENNON: Can nonfiction ever be existential in the sense that you've described it in regard to novels?

MAILER: I think an historian could say, "I start this project with two opposed hypotheses. I'm not sure which is correct. As we explore the material, let me show you the arguments for one, and then for the other. In the course of it, maybe we'll arrive at more of an answer than I have now." Although, to bring that off in truly sustained form is so dangerous, and would so violate the canons of the profession of history, which insist that you go for one stance, not two, that it doesn't often happen. It would tend to agitate exactly what disturbs most people about history in the first place which is that they learn somewhere between high school and college — or is it between graduate school and life? — that history is not history, but a series of immensely sober novels written by men who often don't have large literary talents, and have less to say about the real world than novelists. That's a disturbing discovery. That historians are not dealing with fact, but with the hypothesis they developed in relation to a series of isolated data. The desire to make these facts glow as facets in a mosaic that will enable us to perceive the past is not often done. Once we come to realize that no historians do it more closely than novelists, then all history becomes a novel. Just as any novel is the history of the working of one man's imagination, and so is a real historical artifact to illumine a period for us.

LENNON: How have the metaphors you've used changed over the years?

MAILER: I can tell you a story on that. I had a dear friend, Charlie Devlin, who helped me greatly with *The Naked and the Dead,* and in fact was the model, considerably removed, for the character named McLeod in *Barbary Shore.* Charlie was a quiet saturnine Irishman who was living in a small rooming house where I took a cubicle to finish *The Naked and the Dead.* We used to have long literary conversations. At a certain point I showed him *The Naked and the Dead.* He tore it apart. He was a severe critic. He said, "It's a better book than I thought it would be, but you have no gift for metaphor." Then he said, "Metaphor reveals a man's character, and his true grasp of life. To the degree that you have no metaphor, you are an impoverished writer, and have lived no life." I never forgot this lecture and began to work with might and main on my metaphors. But I can't tell you how they've changed.

LENNON: Many of your characters over the years have carried on negotiations with evil — Marion Faye, D. J., Rojack — I take it that you would not agree with Hannah Arendt on the essential banality of evil?

MAILER: I wouldn't agree with Hannah Arendt at all, not at all. Of course, she can make a case. There are any number of prodigiously evil people who have, from the novelist's point of view, disappointing exteriors. Eichmann, superficially speaking, was a little man, an ordinary man in appearance and vulgar and dull, but to assume therefore that evil itself is banal, strikes me as an exhibition of a prodigious poverty of imagination. You know, one of the paradoxes I always found in the liberal temperament is that they are immensely worshipful of Freud — even though most of his ideas are antipathetic to the notion of liberalism itself. But they go to Freud. The reason is that he is so reductive. Liberals don't like to believe in the vast power of the unconscious, in evil of true murderousness, residing in the most ordinary people. To mistake the surface for the reality, is to perform the fundamental liberal reflex. In effect, liberals are always saying, "I don't see God, so why do you assume God exists?" Out of that has come I think their present bankruptcy. Liberalism has no exciting ideas to offer. I think this enervation comes because it has not been able to deal with the most haunting question of the twentieth century, which is not communism, but nazism. It can't come near to understanding this incredible phenomenon that took over a country of the most decent, hardworking, and *clean* people in the world, this incredible phenomenon of a fascism that went far beyond the normal bounds of totalitarianism into the most extraordinary and despicable extermination of vast numbers of peoples. And this, coming out of a nation which had always been tremendously law-abiding, suggested that the unconscious was truly a hideous place. Liberals, unable to weave that thought into their philosophy, were happy to welcome Hannah Arendt's phrase. But I think to speak of the banality of evil is precisely to point us further in the wrong direction.

LENNON: Didn't Gary Gilmore's story have characteristics that are relevant to this?

MAILER: Probably. I was captured by how complex he was. It seemed to me that it's not the banality or the brutality of evil with which we have to contend, but its complexity, that is, the similarity of evil in others to ourselves. As I got to know Gilmore, and I came to know him better than I know almost anyone in my life,

I began to see that he was a man easily as complex as myself. Naturally, I've always thought of myself as being fairly complicated. Somewhere, in there, I realized that being a murderer was not a final factor, and shouldn't stop all thought. Once we allow ourselves to see Gilmore in his contradictions, the fact that he is a murderer is significant, let's say it's as much as one-quarter of his personality while the potential murderer in each of us might be only one sixteenth or one sixty-fourth of our personality, but fundamentally he is still more like us than unlike us. That is why I wanted to write the book in this way, with its slow accumulation of detail.

LENNON: You didn't have any final judgments on Gilmore?

MAILER: I started with many more opinions than I ended with. I may not be a good intellectual, but my tendency is to create intellections. I put them on like adhesive plasters. In this case I was pulling off the plasters. As I got deeper and deeper into what his nature might be, I decided that every concept I had about Gilmore proved inadequate. So I wanted the reader to confront the true complexity of a human personality that can come from studying one man close enough. The fact that he was a murderer made my task more easy because we're all fascinated with killers. But any person studied in that depth would prove fascinating. It's Flaubert's old idea. You can take any soul alive, including that simple servant girl he wrote about, and make them incredible if you get to know them well enough.

LENNON: *Of Women and Their Elegance* explores Marilyn Monroe's mind and speculates on her ideas, character, obsessions and desires, but does it by way of her inner voice, precisely what you chose not to do for Gilmore. Why? Is Marilyn Monroe less complex than Gilmore?

MAILER: No. A writer has to be ready to gamble when he enters someone's mind. So long as you stay outside, your characters retain a certain integrity, novelistically speaking. There is a mystery about them, a resonance. We can walk around such characters with the same respect we offer people who have a presence in a room. Part of the meaning of charisma is that we don't know the intimate nature of the human force we're dealing with. So, sometimes characters in novels radiate more energy when we don't enter their mind. It is one of the techniques a novelist acquires instinctively — don't enter your protagonist's mind until you have something to say about the interior that's more interesting than the reader's suppositions. The fatal error is to jump in too quickly and then offer banal material. That's the worst of best-sellerdom. Second-rate readers enjoying the insights of second-rate writers.

LENNON: Robert Lucid, the literary critic, once wrote that your writing was based on an implicit — you could almost say, magical — promise to connect the world of Freud with the world of Marx, the public world of politics with the private world of dreams and hallucinations. You called it a "radical bridge." Are you still as committed to this as you were in 1957?

MAILER: I'm no longer particularly interested in Freud. I don't say this disrespectfully. I think Freud had a great deal to say about the nature of the psyche in the nineteenth century. I believe his final importance in intellectual history will be that he gave us more insight into the late nineteenth century than anyone but Marx. Freud is the key to understanding how people put up with the particular kind of lives they led in the 1880s, 1890s, and early 1900s, very much locked up, terribly overstuffed, terrible formal lives. Yet, those lives had a considerable amount of power and energy. In those days the psyche was used like a plumbing system. People were accustomed to living under high pressure. That's not what we have now. Today we know a world in which people act out their anxieties and look to explanations for their conduct all the time. Freud is really not adequate any longer. Marx, for vastly more complex reasons, is also not adequate any longer, not wholly adequate, because corporate capitalism adapted to Marx via Keynes and practically wrapped themselves around some of his ideas. So I don't try to create a bridge from Marx to Freud anymore. I'm not certain I could have.

LENNON: How about other worlds, though? How about the public world of politics and economics, and the private interior world of individuals — hallucinations, surrealism, dream? What about those two worlds? Hasn't your writing always been trying to bridge the inner and outer, public and private?

MAILER: Yes. Always trying. There is a bad sentence I wrote years ago: "Until every manifestation of society from ukase to kiss is comprehended, we will be nowhere." Something of the sort. A most unpleasant sound, "ukase to kiss." I was trying too hard. It was in "The White Negro" and I wrote it at a time when I was coming to realize that everything in society from the largest social institution to those private and intimate personal moments, and the deepest mystical moments such as the onset of death, might all be seen in their connections if one had the courage to begin. In that sense, I'm still trying. But I've come to realize that the task is enormous. Of course, I grew up under the shadow of Marx and Freud. Both men, independently, created an entire world system. They had a vision of all existence. That impressed me immensely. I was nothing if not intellectually ambitious when I was young and wanted to come up with a similar vision that would comprehend everything. By now I've come to realize that it is not only enormously difficult but that I don't have the intellectual discipline to begin to do anything remotely of that sort. But one tries to do one's best with what one's got. I'm still attempting to connect up what I can. Because I do think it's important. Until we understand the ways in which the authorities manipulate us, that is, the ways in which we are obliged to lead our lives in ways we don't particularly enjoy, until we understand all those reasons why so many of us feel dead inside so much of the time, and recognize how much of that is not our lack of imagination but the product of vast institutional systems of greed and injustice that we are schooled to perceive as rather benign manifestations, we are nowhere. The only way I can tell that something terrible is going on is that I feel a little duller than I ought to. Very often that's the end of a very long chain, you might say, of socially intended processes that keeps us malleable, amenable, and short on such powerful emotions as outrage at injustice. In that sense, I'm still trying to find the roots, trace it out, bring in the ultimate indictment against all that's awful and evil in society.

LENNON: That is still a radical bridge, isn't it?

MAILER: Yes, it's just that I don't have these two marvelous mountains — Marx and Freud — any longer. I'm somewhere tracking around in the old lakebeds, kicking up a lot of dust.

LENNON: So you would say that your writing now is less of an exploration than it used to be?

MAILER: Less of an exploration and more of an occupation of territories I reconnoitered years ago. Twenty years ago my mind was so active, I couldn't keep up with it. I had perceptions of all kinds into all sorts of endeavor. I think, not to compare myself, but I believe the same thing happened to Zola. He spoke about how when he was young his thoughts would come so quickly that his hand could not keep up with them as he wrote. As he grew older, the thoughts slowed down, but that was all right, because his hand could now write as fast as his thought. It was the perfect rate. Something of the same sort has happened to me. I now put leaves on the bare branches. It's more satisfying but not as heady as it once was. I'm not as interesting to myself as I used to be.

LENNON: But you've got the card file of all the old ideas to go back to.

MAILER: Well, I live with the old ideas. Part of it is natural. They were so startling when they first came to me that I had to inhabit them, had to grow with them. Maybe I'm bragging, but I think I have a coherent philosophy. I believe we could start talking about virtually anything, and before we were done I could connect our subject to almost anything in my universe.

LENNON: The great book that you hope to write, will that require some new ideas or are you going to be able to use the old ones, the old system, the old philosophy?

MAILER: If I can bring off this three-part novel I'm talking about, I will have to get into places I've never been before. And I'll have to come up with new ideas. I'll have to be bigger and better than I've ever been before. So it is not at all certain to me that I can bring it off. I'm not laying odds.

LENNON: You're off to a hell of a good start.

MAILER: With the Egyptian novel? I hope I am. Practically no one has seen the book, you know.

LENNON: I've heard a few people say it's an amazing work.

MAILER: Well, it's amazing. I mean, chapter for chapter there's extraordinary stuff in it. The question is whether it will hold up. It's one thing to write wonderful chapters, but a great book has to live in other people's minds and change their lives. This book is so ambitious, it's absolutely beyond my measure of anticipation.

After I finish the Egyptian novel, I've then got a second book I want to do about a spaceship in the future, maybe two or three centuries from now, and I'm appalled by the difficulties of the task. I'm going to have to become familiar with science fiction, which I've never read, and get up on the most advanced astro-physics that we have available now. It will be a difficult study for me. Then I'll have to throw that stuff away after I absorb it. The only value it will have for my novel is that the narrator of my book will be able to say, "Yes, back in the twentieth century they believed this was true about the universe. How wrong they were!" That book is going to be staggeringly difficult. Then, of course, the third book, which I look forward to, if I ever get to it, will be contemporary. I've got a couple of tricks up my sleeve that I can't talk about, ways of tying together the Egyptian novel, the novel of the spaceship in the future, and the contemporary book.

So that they will all truly be three parts of the same novel, but in the way a tree might have three trunks growing out of a common root. Or, like the mythical phallus of Osiris which presented itself with three prongs.

1980

A Little
on Novel-Writing

An Interview with Joseph McElroy
and His Writing Class at Columbia

❧

NORMAN MAILER: It might be useful to talk about the practical problems involved in writing a novel, by which I mean the set of psychological stances that you get into in the course of working on one book for a year or two. I remember when I was in college and writing a novel, the great problem I had was (I ran into a phrase by Henry James) "the keeping-up." It's a problem you face when you're young. The novel tends to change too quickly, which is one of the reasons why people in college often tend to write short stories and stay away from longer fiction. Good short story writers often blow up when they start a novel. They'll have a good first chapter, but the second chapter just seems to go off, and they never get it back.

That made me think of the different states I was in when I started each work. Why do I as a voice disappear in one book and appear in another? I found writing some kinds of books to call for this peculiar business of focusing your ego so it becomes literally the hot, burning, highly focused light that underwrites your style.

In other works, your ego tends to disappear completely. You're present as a gentle voice that seems to come in from over the hill — the type of voice that inhabits the third person in most good novels.

In talking about this question of ego and lack of ego, let me make a preface: for reasons that were not very dramatic, I stopped drinking about eight months ago. It's sort of interesting not drinking. I've never been psychoanalyzed, and I thought, this is the closest I'll ever get to it. I know my idea of myself kept changing every day or two. I found that I sort of lost my sense of identity, and didn't know anymore quite who I was in the way that I used to have certain definite assumptions about who I might be. This was sufficiently interesting so that I still haven't gone back to drinking. Because my idea of myself keeps changing. In a way novel-writing is analogous to that — you keep discovering new facets. When you're working on a novel, a variety of motives arise in yourself that shift your sense of identity. That is, honorable reasons and ignoble reasons are both feeding the work. In effect, you have to be writing the book because it's good for you personally, as well as, ideally, for society (or at least your idea of what's good for society).

Apart from that, there are times when one's identity as an author becomes pressing. It's crucial to have some idea then of your own specific density in the social world. How do you impinge on other people? As a result, almost obligatorily, you have to write a novel that has a great emphasis upon the self.

The act of writing has many purposes and many motives, but one of them is a search for one's own increasing sanity. By that I mean one's own increasing effectiveness in the world. Most people start writing out of the curled-up reflex that they're not quite able to contend with the world. They also write in order to become more attractive in the world, more powerful.

JOSEPH MCELROY: To get your own back, Orwell says.

MAILER: Yes. There are those periods when there's a vast absorption in oneself, and in a way, the nicest and happiest and most elegant solution to that is to write a novel in which the protagonist is close to yourself. If you can keep one hand on that high overhead line, that high-voltage line of irony, so that you don't take yourself too seriously, you get to that wonderful land between high seriousness and self-ridicule that is perfectly balanced. Then you've got something awfully good. When you abase and attack yourself, or take yourself too seriously, you have a disaster. You need a marvelous internal navigator to keep bringing you back on course in such a book.

Then there are books where you can no longer deal with yourself — it's too exhausting. You want a vacation from yourself. Sometimes one wants to live like a ghost. Some writers stay in one vein all their lives; other writers keep going back and forth between personal and objective books. You have people who always write out of their own voice, like Hemingway. Then you have writers who never step into their work, like Tolstoy* and James Michener.

STUDENT: You were saying at your reading last night, that at a certain point in your life you went out in the world instead of using that energy in your writing. Could you talk about that?

MAILER: I think most writers do have this problem, particularly if they arrive early. Those of you who don't, can have the fine consolation that your experience will at least remain your own; and that if you have a friend, he's real. People who notice you when you are unknown, notice you because you are in fact a lively protagonist in a given situation, and not because you're walking into the room with a reputation.

The problem of going out and searching for experience, I think, is true for very young writers who just don't have enough to write about. There comes a point where you say, "I want to be a writer, I feel all the equipment of a writer. I feel the livid intelligence of a writer, but I don't really know enough." This is where journalism rears its ugly head. It's very hard to enter strange places and learn a lot about them unless you have clout. Kids get into journalism because the moment they flash a card that says they're a bona fide reporter, people start talking to them. Of course it's a false experience. Hopefully, you develop the sense how to filter this experience, and correct it, refract it into what the experience might have been like if you hadn't had this peculiar advantage of being a journalist.

I discovered this all by myself when I started doing journalism, and realized it was a marvelous way for me to work. It was vastly easier than trying to write novels, and I was discouraged with the difficulty of writing them at that point. I had run into this business of trying to tell a good story and yet say wonderful things about the nature of the world and society, touch all the ultimates, and yet at the same time, have it read like speed. There are so many pitfalls to this. I always had a terrible time with the story. My stories were always ending up begrounded. There I'd be, in the middle of the dunes, no gas in the tank. I loved journalism because it gave me the story, which I'd always been weakest in. Then I discovered that this was the horror of it. Audiences liked

---

* An irresponsible remark! I must have been thinking of "The Death of Ivan Ilyich" rather than *War and Peace*.

it better. They'd all been seeing the same story you'd been seeing, and they wanted interpretation. It was those critical faculties that were being called for, rather than one's novelistic gifts. Under all those temptations, I must say I succumbed, and I spent a good many years working at the edge of journalism, because it was so much easier.

I was asked last night what I'd do if I had it all to do over again, and I said that if I'd had more discipline, I would probably have tried to stick with the novel. Still journalism has its own disciplines. Ideally, you must not only describe the event and bring your own perception to it, but say to the reader, "This is the kind of man or woman I am. This is the way I perceive the event. Now you, having been given me first, and then the event, can see around me into the event, and come away with your own conclusions. They might be different from mine."

In a novel, you do try to create something that exists separately from yourself, even if it's a manifest with yourself as the protagonist. Ideally, at a certain point that novel ought to be able to be separated from you.

STUDENT: How do you write as a novelist when, on the one hand, you have this story that's already been told, and you have all this research, and then you have the act of writing?

MAILER: The trick, as I found for myself, is just to keep from doing it all at once. When I work on a novel — I've had a novel working for years — I don't like to know the end. I'm happier finding things out at the point of the pencil. I think that if you solve the problem of how a chapter's going to end in the shower, then you're not as well off as if you get it while writing. I felt this with *The Executioner's Song.* While I knew the story, I saw this as a hazard. I wanted the book to read as if we did not know the ending. I didn't want to be aware of too many future details, because this would tend to make me curve what was happening to my characters at the place where I had them. I would understand too well their relation to what was going to happen later.

STUDENT: When you're writing about a story that's superficially very well known, there must be some very private experience about what goes into the writing of it.

MAILER: Well, I think *The Executioner's Song*, more than any other book I've ever done, was an exercise in craft. I've never felt close to it. I will say that there were many pitfalls to be avoided in the writing of it, and it did require those many years of experience. What you need is a tremendous amount of lore that'll let you know where all the pitfalls are, and enable you to avoid them.

MCELROY: Can we talk a bit about an earlier book, *Why Are We in Vietnam?* How did you feel when you were writing it?

MAILER: Well, it's the perfect foil to *The Executioner's Song.* I must start with an excursion to the side in answer to your question. Years ago I knew a lot of painters, abstract expressionists, young ones, and I had just begun to understand most of the work they were doing. You'd come in and one of them would have done about twenty window shades. It looked to my untutored eye as if they'd thrown some paint on these window shades and then let it drip down. I knew one of the painters better than the others, and I remember she said, "That's awfully interesting work." I said, "Interesting, what do you mean, interesting? It's horrible." She said, "What he's done is very valuable," and I said, "Why?," and she said, "Well, I'm glad he's done it, because now I don't have to do it." That was the period when they were truly exploring every last way you could put color on a surface, and so she was happy with it, because it saved her some work — she didn't have to go in that direction. You'll find very often in writing, that in the beginning, you have to go in certain directions to find out if they're attractive to you, and if you can do something with them, or also just whether you like them or not. I don't think I could have written *The Executioner's Song* if I hadn't written *Why Are We in Vietnam?*, because there I had the experience of expressing myself without a backward look. I think that *Why Are We in Vietnam?* is interesting to me, because I was able this once to transmute myself and create a somewhat ongoing, rampant, inflamed, sort of mad ego. If there are any forces in the cosmos that ever step in and give a helping hand to a writer, I got it right there.

The Executioner's Song, on the other hand, was another kind of gift, and I was delighted to have been given it. So in effect, two of the best books I've done are not mine. One, from the inside, and one, from the outside. They couldn't be more different, those two books, in every way.

STUDENT: Is your new Egyptian novel mostly research, or is it more of a creative process?

MAILER: There's an awful lot of research, but the trick is to digest it. The most difficult thing about writing an historical novel is to avoid that awful stance where you say, "Hello, I'm Saint-Simon and I'm at the court of Louis XIV and Madame de Maintenon is very angry this morning." You have to get to that point of view in your writing where you say to yourself, "Madame de Maintenon does not quite know that she's the Madame de Maintenon that we know through Saint-Simon. She sees herself as someone other." You have to decide how she sees herself. That's what you're trying to get in an historical novel, and it's very difficult. Anachronisms come in with every phrase. Reading from my Egyptian book aloud last night, I kept thinking, oh my God, there are so many things I like or don't like in terms of style; I felt certain words were reasonable for an Egyptian of the Twentieth Dynasty and others weren't at all. Cleaning up the style is crucial to writing an historical novel. I did a book on Marilyn Monroe which came out last fall, and in that the writing was nothing much — it was easy to write, a question of feeling like a medium — hearing her voice and writing it. Once you begin to discover the ways in which characters talk like themselves and the way they talk like you, you try to write it in their voice, not your own voice. It takes a certain patience to go through and keep weeding out all those traces that don't belong. The problem is magnified in an historical novel.

STUDENT: You once said that form was a substitute for talent or style.

MAILER: I think it's a substitute for inspiration. A perfect example of this is the new journalism. Here the form is delivered to you by the plot of the event. It's a great substitute for the talent to conceive a good story. Of course you still have to flesh it out, but at least the event happened. In novel-writing you have to deal more with time. For instance, putting a story in the first person immediately takes care of the present. I've always found it much easier to write in the first person than in the third person, because in the third person you're making certain philosophical assumptions that the reader may not accept. It is tricky. You're assuming you're God, or some extraordinary observer. In *The Executioner's Song*, the biggest difficulty I had was to get myself knuckled down to the simple point of telling that story flatly, blankly, in the third person.

MCELROY: I think you're right about the first person — the reader will give you that much.

MAILER: Yes, writing in the first person you don't have to jump from one head to another. As I was saying, in *The Executioner's Song*, since I wanted to move through everybody's head, and make no pretty bones about it, I was paralyzed for a month. I just couldn't do it. Finally I thought, "Well, you're going to have to make the jump." To this day I feel uneasy about it. I feel I've violated the fundamental intregrity of the novel.

One thing though, for me, about many novels — I think you have to work as if you're a farmer, and rotate your crops. If you write a novel that's factual and realistic and big, awfully close to what happened, then it's probably a good idea that your next novel be as fanciful as possible. That way you're rotating the crops in your brain.

MCELROY: Do you ever write short stories?

MAILER: Not often anymore, and I have something not awfully attractive to say about that. After you become a working writer, make your living as a writer, then what you write, to a larger extent than you realize, is determined by whether you make your living at it. The sad thing about writing short stories is that you can't. I don't think there are more than four or five writers of short stories in this country who actually do survive that way year after year.

STUDENT: Can we get back to inspiration? It sounds like if something inspires you, because it inspires you, you're willing to justify it ideologically.

MAILER: If you find some theme that keeps you working, don't question it. Let that theme be sufficient to fuel your work. If you start using the value judgments of others, you're never going to get much done. The thing to remember is that there's nobody anymore, not even the President, who can tell us how to live. Nobody knows the answer. If I find something is stimulating me and arousing my energy, that's fine, I'll trust it. If you're a serious young writer and find you are writing, my God, don't listen to what anyone else says, write your book. There probably is a deeper truth than you'll ever know in the fact that you're able to work so well. Of course, you could be writing in absolutely the wrong direction. You could be doing a dreadful book. You could be, let's take an extreme example, flirting with something that justifies Hitler, and you say to yourself, "What am I doing? I'm a monster. Why am I writing this book?" Who knows — in the process of creating such a work you might reawaken the attention of civilization to the fact that they're getting kind of casual, and complacent about Hitler. You see, you won't know the results of your action. The greatest vanity, the thing that has poisoned Marxist literature for decades, is that they assume writers can affect the population profoundly in ways that are foreseeable, and therefore writers should work like scientists.

But, no matter what you find yourself writing about, if it's giving you enough energy to continue then the work bears a profound relationship to you at that point and so you don't question it.

STUDENT: Could you talk a bit about your early career, and the difficulties of writing your first novel, *The Naked and the Dead?*

MAILER: That was probably the easiest and the happiest book I ever wrote. When it came out I was twenty-five. I did it in about fifteen months. I was filled with the war, I'd just come back. This was a relatively peaceful period. The only anxiety I suffered while writing was that my opinion of the book was much higher than it deserved to be. I was young and I thought, "This is the greatest book since *War and Peace.* Maybe it's better." I used to walk around in a rage after reading the *New York Times Book Review,* because of some awful book that was being celebrated. I'd go to my editor and say, "Do you people realize that if they don't treat this book properly I'm going to be forced to go out and write potboilers?" I took myself very seriously. Once, before I'm done, I'd like to get another book that comes through me so quickly. I was getting five good ideas for every bad one, and happily I was oblivious to the faults of the book. At the time of *The Naked and the Dead* I was writing in a style that had very little literary merit to it. The force of the book prevailed over the style. I was lucky. If I'd been even a fraction more concerned with the merits of style, the book would have slowed up and I wouldn't have been able to write it.

STUDENT: What do you think of the way the book turned out — the death of Hearn? It was sure a big surprise.

MAILER: I haven't thought of that in years. Really, it is a shocking death. I must say I stole that directly from E. M. Forster, in *The Longest Journey.* He created a character who was most alive for the reader, and then destroyed him on the next page. Like a rifle shot. You get an idea what a gun is like at that point. In my book it may have been too big a price to pay, because the denouement of the novel was sacrificed. I don't think I was aware of the size of the problem. Today I'd be much more alert to that. If I did the book over again today, I might have kept Hearn alive until the very end, and it might have been a phonier book as a result. It might have been more effective but less true. One of the things you always have trouble with when you talk about "true" or "not true" is, of course, the relative truth of the novel. In a way, if you get a fairly good novel going, then you have a universe functioning, and this universe lives or does not live in relation to its own scheme of cause and effect, of reaction and response. In Kafka's writing, he creates worlds that are absolutely true. You can say practically every sentence in a Kafka story is true to the story.

Looking back on it, I can give you a good and bad motive that I had for killing Hearn at that point. The good motive was that it seemed to me that it was about as powerful a way to show what death is like in war as anything I could do in that book. The shoddy motive was I wasn't altogether sure in my heart that I knew what to do with him, or knew how to bring him off.

MCELROY: You were suspicious even then for the long-range plans of a given book? That is, you'd let where you were going at a given point decide what to do next, right?

MAILER: I think that I truly work on impulse in all of my writing. That's why I don't like to plan too far ahead. It makes it almost impossible to have one of your characters go through a dipsy-doodle bend, because it's going to violate your larger scheme. It's better if the larger scheme comes into focus at the very last moment.

STUDENT: Back to some of the advice you were giving young writers. It seems you're saying that if it feels good, go with it and don't listen to what everybody says. Back when you were young and you were plowing through your stuff, were you aware or was there a mentor around to tell you that if it felt good, go with it; or did you have your doubts and just write your way through it? Didn't you sometimes get your head turned around by all the different forces working on you? Or were you aware, maybe instinctively, of what to do?

MAILER: I think I probably had a certain urgency about writing, because it seemed to me that it was probably the only thing I could do well. There is a great tendency then to follow your own instincts, because that's all you've got. Let me amplify this. Your instinct could be dead wrong. In other words, you could write a book with a powerful sense of inner conviction. You could finish writing it, and a year or two later, look at it and say, "How could I have so deluded myself? This is awful." This inner experience, this instinct can betray you, but you still have to go with it. Very often the instinct sees some light at the end of the tunnel, but that's because you've been trapped in a situation where your creative energies just can't get together. Now, there's become a way to work. You may be writing out some very bad tendencies in yourself, but this can be good, too. Feel happy because (thank God) soon you're going to be done with that stupid side of yourself. That's what the enthusiasm can be about.

STUDENT: How do you go about rewriting?

MAILER: That's where your experience comes in. The more you rewrite, the better you get at it. There comes a point when you may feel on the declining side of your powers. At this point, if you've become one of the best editors in town, then those declining powers will seem much less weak to others than to yourself. That's because you know how to get the maximum out of what you have done. The only way to do this when you're young is to go through your work in every mood. You have to have the courage to look at it when you're in a terrible mood, ready to destroy it. If at that point something still comes through, then at least you have the assurance that it has to be pretty good, at least to you. And then, of course, it's very good to read things at the top of your feelings, way up, to see what the maximum is. If nothing else, all this gives you tolerance for the extraordinary spectrum of reactions you get in the classroom. You realize that the people that hate your work aren't necessarily evil, and the people who love your stuff are not altogether illustrious.

STUDENT: What happens when you find yourself lacking in inspiration or impulse? Do you utilize a problem-solving measure to create inspiration?

MAILER: Well, sometimes you're in the middle of an interesting chapter, but you don't know what the denouement is. You've got interesting people and have aroused certain expectations in your reader and now you don't know what to do with it all. That is the ongoing problem of doing a novel from day to day. As I said, James used that expression, "the keeping-up." How do you keep the level up in such a way that you don't get too dramatic or, equally, don't dissipate a good opportunity? You sit there and you have to solve that problem. Practice is a big part of it. There's a sense of inner timing that develops over the years. There is also the key word, taste. Taste becomes refined. Of course, it can get refined to the point where it ceases to exist.

STUDENT: You're a controversial public figure. I wonder how you feel about your past.

MAILER: After a while you walk around your own life as though it were a piece of sculpture. It depends on where you're looking at it from. Are you thinking of it from the point of view of your work, or your children? Actually, I find I think less and less about myself as I get older. You begin to have the feeling, "Well, I may only have another so many years to write, and write halfway well," and you tend to get more serious. You get practical about your life, and realize that there's going to be more and more work, and less and less fun as you go along. You say, "I'll think about that old part of my life when I'm writing about it, and if I never write about it, I'll never think about it again."

1981

To Pontificate on America and Europe

An Interview with Barbara Probst Solomon

ᔰ

BARBARA PROBST SOLOMON: When Hemingway and Miller went to live and write in Europe, writers were not like governments, they were not nationalistic; they had something to say to each other. Americans and Europeans don't talk to each other very much at this point. Do you feel our novelists have gone in very different directions?

NORMAN MAILER: Yes, I think so.

SOLOMON: European writers have been more influenced by developments in linguistics. American innovators — and you have been a leading force — have gone in another direction. What do you think about this?

MAILER: I think of Borges, who is doing something else altogether. I don't know enough about South America to decide how much Borges speaks for Argentina and South America — but finally, I think of Borges as European because to do what Borges does you need a culture that is profound. Almost none of us in America has that kind of culture. It's possible Saul Bellow is the best read of American novelists; John Barth, maybe. I can think of a few others but none of them has been able to take that culture and use it forcefully in their work. It hardly matters that Bellow is conversant with probably all the great and medium great and small great writers of the Western world since Plato and Aristotle. It doesn't enrich his work, not the way Borges' culture does. Borges poses for us, I think, the difficulty of comprehending reality. He

183

shows us that as we approach reality we are writing scenarios that are the equivalent of propositions and hypotheses in physics. That is, they are correct until the evidence subverts them. But even as they are being subverted we learn a great deal because the next hypothesis, ideally, should be superior.

So in Borges you have this wonderful business of an immensely elaborate hypothesis destroyed by the one fact that turns it inside out. There is this marvelously sinewy dialectical vision of the interplay between culture and history, the two almost being — not artifacts — but separate organisms. Borges reveals to us his immensely vivid inner life which I think is all one finally cares about in another author. It is what I should be able to give others in my own writing. If our inner lives are more alive, we are more able to stand proof against the attacks of the world. And by now the attacks of the world upon our psyche are not so much aggressive as subtle, insidious — we're leached out. We're not destroyed from without, we are sucked out. Our spiritual souls, our social souls, are sucked out of us by the mass media, by information retrievable. I think Borges is the best when it comes to fighting that. Try putting Borges in a computer.

Now, the ways in which the Europeans have been going at it, have come out of a profound weariness with the novel, with plot, with all the impedimenta of writing a book. Everything that is detestable in the best-selling novel comes to visit you every time you try to tell a story. It's getting harder and harder. So you look for ways to get away from it. I suppose I've looked to other fields. To journalism. To historical events that I could write about as they were occurring. Because it's another way of apprehending reality. My fundamental stance in all this is that the attempt to apprehend reality is what is interesting. Because we learn from the attempt. We can't learn that much from the final product. All we can do is argue about how successful it is.

SOLOMON: You wrote, in *The Armies of the Night*, that what saved America was our humor, the belly laugh, "The noble common man was obscene as an old goat and his obscenity was what saved him." The guy who says, "Man, I just managed to take me a noble shit." That cadence is at the heart of the American vernacular. Do you feel all this European weariness comes from their essentially non-democratic society? Where writers feel their connection to the upper rather than lower reaches of society?

MAILER: I think it has a great deal to do with it. I think it's also impossible to live with a culture as rich as the culture of the Western world without being aghast at the poverty of one's ability to write about it. Americans have a saving instinct — we're not that near to European high culture. Sooner or later we suffer from having ignored it; we feel the paucity of our own culture, but at least we're not living in the shadow of the great beauty. Which is the shade, let us say, that sits over the light of European literary endeavor. Americans can live and work on a different street. We don't have to contemplate the beauty every day. In America one can still have the illusion that one is doing something brand new. One can feel like a pioneer.

But it's getting harder; we didn't start with much culture and we never achieved a truly rich American marrow. We're now in terrible trouble because we're getting to the point where we are destroying our culture at a much greater rate than we are creating it. And on top of that, we are exporting it to the rest of the world. Our heritage is in danger of arriving on the main historical stage all but cultureless; and for some time Europe has been attracted by the novelty of America's cultureless culture — taking our architecture, our superhighways, our plastics, our McDonald's, our Coca-Cola and all of it. They're destroying their culture. But in Europe, at least, they have something interesting to burn. So it's going to take them much longer. I make a prediction that European literature is going to get vastly interesting a little further down the road about the time that a great deal of European culture is being destroyed. I think that talented European writers are going to be struck by the tension between the value of what is being destroyed and the ferment of the destruction itself. Some very interesting works are going to come out of it.

SOLOMON: So you think the balance of tension is going to shift because of their fascination with America?

MAILER: Not so much because of America. I think it's going to shift because they won't be living in the shade of their culture any longer. That culture is going to be destroyed to a degree where Europeans will be able to breathe again. At a terrible price to that culture. But they'll be able to breathe again and, of course, breathing again, they're going to value that culture for the first time in decades, rather than feel awe, resentment and reverence for it.

SOLOMON: You were influenced by a European, Jean Malaquais?

MAILER: Yes, very much.

SOLOMON: In *The Armies of the Night*, which was published in '68, you wrote, "Communism would continue to produce heretics and great innovators just so long as it expanded. Between Poland and India, Prague and Bangkok was a diversity of primitive lore which would jam every fine gear of the Marxist." You seem to be proved right.

MAILER: Yes, perhaps.

SOLOMON: That doesn't interest you?

MAILER: I think it would be more Malaquais' idea than mine. Jean Malaquais is the first person I knew who talked seriously and coherently about the inner contradictions of Soviet communism. That is, the very forces that would ultimately destroy communism. But the language in *The Armies of the Night* is not his but mine. I don't know that Malaquais pays as much attention as I do to primitive lore. I can't take credit for the idea, but feel satisfaction as I read it.

SOLOMON: Yes, but you can take credit for the ideas that you choose. We're always choosing somebody else's ideas.

MAILER: I think in choosing some of Malaquais' ideas, I chose well. Better than I usually do.

SOLOMON: In *Armies,* when you are in your Washington hotel room in the Hay-Adams, you reflect on federalist architecture, and suddenly what swam in front of my mind was *The Federalist Papers, Democracy,* and *The Education of Henry Adams.* In that section you mention his influence on you. Did you mean his novel *Democracy* or *The Education of Henry Adams*?

MAILER: The influence of Adams on *The Armies of the Night* was most peculiar. To the best of my recollection, I never read much Adams. I know for certain that I read one long chapter of *The Education of Henry Adams* in my freshman reader at Harvard. I remember thinking at the time, "What an odd thing to do, to write about yourself in the third person. Who is this fellow, Henry Adams, talking about himself as Adams," and being struck with it in that mildly irritable way freshmen have of passing over extraordinary works of literature. It's possible that I then read more of *The Education of Henry Adams* sometime in my freshman or sophomore year although I wouldn't claim that I did. I never wrote about Adams, never thought about him particularly, would never have mentioned his name as one of the writers that were important to me, and yet in *Armies,* one starts reading it, and immediately one says — even I said — "My God, this is pure Henry Adams." What the hell is going on here? It's an absolute take-off, as if I were the great-grandson of Henry Adams. You don't have to posit any other influence but Adams for *The Armies of the Night.*

So look how peculiar is influence: Adams was stuck in my unconscious as a possibility, the way it happens with painters much more than with writers. A painter can look at a particular Picasso, or Cézanne and say to himself, "That's the way to do it." But the work might not pop out for twenty or thirty years. When it does, they say, "Oh yes, there was a Picasso I saw at MOMA twenty-five years ago. I always wanted to try a palette of such and such, and I decided to use it here." In effect, that's what happened to me.

SOLOMON: Adams seems to have been one of the few good American writers who thought of putting Washington, D.C. and an American president at the center of a novel — *Democracy.* I thought of this in connection with you — the protagonist discards Washington and ends contemplating Egypt. So I felt that Adams subliminally was reaching to you on all levels.

MAILER: Well, he is and he isn't. I feel absolutely at a loss before Henry Adams. I mean, on the basis of these facts, it's spooky. I didn't know about Egypt, for instance. Yet one of his books ends with a character going there?

SOLOMON: Madeline Lee in *Democracy* gets disgusted with Washington and then goes off to Egypt at the end of the book. You do seem more like Henry Adams' great-grandson at this moment that you do Hemingway's son.

MAILER: Yes, because here I am going off to Egypt . . . for the last ten years.

SOLOMON: Did any of the elasticity of the Jewish historical experience help you make that imaginative leap into Egypt?

MAILER: I don't know why I started writing about Egypt. I've been working on that book off and on for ten years. I feel only now as if I'm slowly beginning to understand it, that is, the Egypt of antiquity. You can very often write well about matters that you don't understand too well. Most of my life I've written in advance of my comprehension of a subject. Often, years later, I would come to understand the material better and be amazed that I could have done it at all when I did. Oddly enough, now that I have the knowledge, I probably couldn't write about it. There's some potentiality in all of us that we tap when we write. The best writing comes out of that. I don't know that the work I'm writing about Egypt now is better than the stuff eight to ten years ago when I knew very little.

Something in me then was drawn toward Egypt although nothing in my past was even remotely related. All my interests are contemporary. I'm certainly not a man of classical education, in relation to most writers not a man with historical concerns. Yet in this Egyptian book I wish nothing in it to be contemporary. And of course it is a totally different culture. It existed long before Jesus, so there's absolutely nothing of a Christian notion of compassion, which is the very center of all Western thought. There is also nothing of the Judaic tradition. At the time I am writing about, the Jews are a tribe of barbarians who occasionally give a little trouble on the borders. Moses comes into the book for a page. He's mentioned as this fellow who went wild out on the Eastern desert and helped some of the Hebrews pull off a massacre and then took off farther east. That's all we know about Moses in my book. I can't answer why I've been so fascinated with Egypt. I sometimes think that I'm attracted to a subject for literary purposes because I know so little about it — except that I have one deep instinct into the subject.

Let me give you an example. It's more fun to pick up a mystery novel and read it, if early in that book you decide that you and the author share a perception that no one else has. Then you are going to get more out of this book than anyone else, even though you know nothing about the material or the crime. I think something of that sort works in historical research. You have to feel that you do know more than the average historian about one aspect of the subject. I think that I felt I knew more about burial customs than the average Egyptologist. Not more about the details of them, which I hadn't learned, then, but more about the reason for them.

SOLOMON: Did you need a subject of the dimension of Egypt to be able to pull yourself away from America? Up until now America has been a big character in your novels.

MAILER: Yes, but I haven't been altogether successful in pulling away. Sometimes I've gotten terribly tired of this Egyptian book because there's nothing to say in it about America today. *The Executioner's Song* was written as a reaction. It allowed me to immerse myself again in daily matters of American life. I went out to Utah, a place whose inhabitants have hardly heard of New York and where they certainly never have heard of me. I learned again how Americans who don't live in the media do in fact live interesting lives and I steeped myself in all the minutiae of American life. When I went back to the Egyptian book, it was with a certain sense of refreshment. There's been this alternation over the last ten years — writing about Egypt and then writing about matters that are very American: Marilyn Monroe, Muhammad Ali, Henry Miller, Gary Gilmore.

SOLOMON: Do you physically *see* Egypt?

MAILER: Yes, oh yes. I see it so clearly that I can't stand going there. I went once for a visit and said, I have to get out of here. Because it was ruining my vision. It had nothing to do with Egypt of antiquity. I got out fast.

SOLOMON: Language has always been very important in your books. What do you hear in the Egyptian book? What vernacular?

MAILER: I've been studying the Egyptian language a little bit, not in a very serious or concerted way, but I've been using an Egyptian dictionary and I find it fascinating. Ancient Egyptian is a wonderful language, a very dialectical language. Often the nearest cousin to a word means the exact opposite. For example: the word for "dung" also means "the bleaching of linen." And you find this all through the language. The word for "magnetism" is also the word for "you." It's a tremendously sensuous language, rather existential. You feel that the ancient Egyptians had already articulated one highly complex and wonderful and rather magical civilization, and yet they were still close to the primitive. Every word in the language is a revelation. Every word is related to every other word in a fashion that we don't have today. Like "you" and "magnetism." The reason the two words were the same is that when people looked at one another they felt the play of forces between them. Today we have that crude expression, "good vibes," but it's a pale reflection of ancient Egyptian.

SOLOMON: Very few novelists, excepting Saul Bellow, seem to write expansive books.

MAILER: Well, it's hard. It's hard to write well on a large subject. Actually, most large subjects are handled by best-selling novelists. They will have a cast of forty or fifty characters. They'll have stories that cover fifty to one hundred years. They'll have a couple of world wars. They'll have startling changes in the lives of several families. The reason they do all that in a hurry is because they can keep their book moving. What characterizes a best-selling novel is that there's nothing in it that you haven't come across before. At least if you're a reader of some experience. Most serious writers tend to work on smaller and smaller canvases and expatiate upon them with more and more clarity. And that's terribly important. At least they're contributing to knowledge rather than adding to the general cultural sludge that lies over everything. So it's very hard to take on a large topic. At the moment the only living writer I can think of who can handle what I've described — forty to fifty characters and one hundred years — is Garcia Márquez. *One Hundred Years of Solitude* is an amazing work. Garcia Márquez succeeds in doing it, but how, I don't know. In my Egyptian novel — although it's very, very long — not that much happens. As I've said before it takes me ten pages to go around a bend in the Nile.

1981

Acknowledgments

✢

"Hip, Hell and the Navigator" by Richard G. Stern originally appeared in *The Western Review*, Winter 1959.

"An Impolite Interview" originally appeared as "An Impolite Interview with Norman Mailer" by Paul Krassner in *The Realist*, No. 40, December 1962.

"Craft and Consciousness" appeared as "An Interview with Norman Mailer" from *Writers at Work: The Paris Review Interviews*, third series, © 1967 by The Paris Review, Inc. Reprinted by permission of Viking Penguin Inc.

"Talking of Violence" by W. J. Weatherby originally appeared in *Twentieth Century*, Winter 1964–1965.

"Vices" originally appeared in *Playboy* Magazine; Copyright © 1967 by Playboy. Reprinted by permission of Playboy.

"Norman Mailer on Science and Art" by David Young originally appeared in *Antaeus*, April 1, 1974.

"In Search of the Devil" excerpted from "The Rolling Stone Interview with Norman Mailer" by Richard Stratton from *Rolling Stone* No. 177, January 2, 1975 and No. 178, January 16, 1975. By Straight Arrow Publishers, Inc. © 1975. All rights reserved. Reprinted by permission.

"Existential Aesthetics: An Interview with Norman Mailer" by Laura Adams originally appeared in *Partisan Review*, No. 2, 1975.

"Marriage" originally appeared as "Mailer on Marriage and Women" by Bernard Farbar in *Viva*, October 1973.

"One-Night Stands" originally appeared as "Norman Mailer on Love, Sex, God and the Devil." Interview by Cathleen Medwick. Courtesy *Vogue*. Copyright © 1980 by The Condé Nast Publications, Inc. Reprinted by permission.

"Ethics and Pornography" by Jeffrey Michelson and Sarah Stone originally appeared in *Puritan*, No. 7, published by Puritan Publishing, Inc., Allentown, Pennsylvania.

"Prisoner of Success" by Paul Attanasio originally appeared in the *Boston Phoenix* on February 24, 1981. Reprinted by permission.

"A Brief Exchange" by Anita Eichholz is excerpted from the transcript of *Norman Mailer: The Sanction to Write*, a documentary film produced by Jeffrey Van Davis. Reprinted by permission.

The four "Munich" interviews by Michael Lennon: "Waste": "An Author's Identity"; "Writers and Boxers"; and "Literary Ambitions" are excerpted from the transcript of *Norman Mailer: The Sanction to Write*, a documentary film produced by Jeffrey Van Davis. Reprinted by permission.

"The Mad Butler" originally appeared as "Creators on Creating: Norman Mailer" by Hilary Mills in *Saturday Review*. Copyright © 1981 by Saturday Review. All rights reserved. Reprinted by permission.

"A Little on Novel-Writing" by Joseph McElroy originally appeared in *Columbia: A Magazine of Poetry and Prose*, No. 6, 1981. The interview was conducted under the auspices of The National Committee for the Literary Arts.

"To Pontificate on America and Europe," originally published as "A Conversation with Norman Mailer," © 1981 by Barbara Probst Solomon, is excerpted from an interview dated July 16, 1981 originally published in *El Pais*, Madrid, on October 4, 1981. Reprinted by permission.